PHILIP LARKIN

Warren Hope

Greenwich Exchange, London

First published in Great Britain in 1997
Reprinted 2002

Philip Larkin © Warren Hope 2002

Printed and bound by Q3 Digital/Litho, Loughborough
Tel: 01509 213456
Typesetting and layout by Albion Associates, London
Tel: 020 8852 4646
Cover design: December Publications, Belfast
Tel: 028 9035 2059

Cover photograph: © University of Hull

Greenwich Exchange Website: www.greenex.co.uk

ISBN 1-871551-35-8

For Bob Barth

Contents

Chronology

9th August 1922

Philip Arthur Larkin born in Coventry, the son of Eva Emily (Day) Larkin and Sydney Larkin, who had married in 1911. Larkin had one sister, Catherine.

1930-1940

Attended preparatory school and grammar school at King Henry VIII School, Coventry. Contributed to *The Coventrian*, the school magazine.

1940-1943

Entered St John's College, Oxford, in October 1940 to read English Language and Literature. Friends at Oxford included Kingsley Amis, who dedicated his novel *Lucky Jim* to Larkin, Bruce Montgomery, who wrote detective novels under the pen name, Edmund Crispin, and dedicated *The Moving Toyshop* to Larkin, and John Wain, the poet and novelist. Found unfit for military service on medical grounds – poor eyesight – in January, 1942. Earned a First Class degree in June 1943.

July to December 1943

Lived with parents in Warwick and worked on poems and his first novel, *Jill*. Became Librarian at Wellington in Shropshire in December.

July 1945

The North Ship, his first collection of poems, published by the Fortune Press.

1946 Assistant Librarian at University College, Leicester, where he met Monica Jones, the woman to whom *The Less Deceived* was dedicated. *Jill*, his first novel, was published by the Fortune Press in October.

1947 *A Girl in Winter*, Larkin's second novel, published by Faber & Faber in February.

1948 Sydney Larkin died on 26th March.

1950 Sub-Librarian at Queen's University, Belfast, where he met Winifred Arnott to whom several poems in *The Less Deceived* are addressed.

1951 *XX Poems* printed privately by Larkin in Belfast.

1953 Some of Larkin's poems selected by John Wain to be read on the BBC.

1954 Five poems by Larkin appeared in *The Fantasy Poets No. 21* published at Oxford. First contribution to *Listen*, magazine edited by George Hartley of the Marvell Press.

1955 Librarian at the University of Hull. *The Less Deceived* published by the Marvell Press.

1961 Larkin began to review jazz records for *The Daily Telegraph*.

1964 *The Whitsun Weddings* published by Faber & Faber.

1965 Awarded the Queen's Gold Medal for Poetry.

1970 *All What Jazz* published by Faber & Faber.

1973 Larkin's anthology, *The Oxford Book of Twentieth Century English Verse*, published by the Clarendon Press.

1974 *High Windows* published by Faber & Faber.

1975 Awarded the CBE.

1976 Awarded the Shakespeare Prize in Hamburg, Germany.

1977   Eva Larkin died on 17th November. 'Aubade' published in *The Times Literary Supplement* in December.

1983   *Required Writing* published by Faber & Faber.

1985   Philip Larkin died on 2nd December in the Hull Nuffield Hospital. He was buried in Cottingham Cemetery.

1 *The Less Deceived*

In the autumn of 1955, a small publisher in a provincial city in the north of England issued a slender volume of poems. The book contained 29 short poems – some of them were only 8 or 10 lines long and none of them ran onto a third page. The author of the poems was a librarian at the local university.

It would not be surprising to learn that the world greeted this event with a politely stifled yawn. Instead, *The Less Deceived* by Philip Larkin became what now has the look of an overnight success – praised by judicious critics and enthusiastically taken up by readers of poetry. What was the basis of that praise and enthusiasm?

Mostly they were based on what Larkin had to say and the way he said it. The post-war world in Britain had been flooded with inflated, rhetorical, neo-Romantic poems, to a large extent imitations of the work of Dylan Thomas, who had died at an early age and under legendmaking circumstances in 1953. Grand gestures in grand language that struck readers as false, hollow, and obscure seemed to be the order of the day in poetry. Larkin's voice, on the other hand, was clear, witty, and understated. This voice found its subjects, for the most part, in the recognisable objects of the actual world and in the way life is lived by so-called ordinary people. The praise of critics and the enthusiasm of readers came in part from a sense of relief. They knew what Larkin was talking about without the need to either rush to a dictionary or to sign up for a course at a university.

The wonder is that both critics and readers were in agreement. The growing tendency throughout the twentieth century had been for critics to explain to readers the significance or importance of poems that readers found difficult or dull or both. On the other hand, critics, as guardians of culture with a capital C, also explained to readers why poems that were once relatively popular – those of some of the Georgian poets, for instance – must now be dismissed as hopelessly naive, simple-minded, and passé. Although Larkin's work quietly and indirectly questioned many of the century's critical assumptions, critics recognised in it a seriousness and a skill that would not allow them to ignore it.

I

One of the short poems in *The Less Deceived,* 'Coming', helps to make these qualities of Larkin's work clear. This little lyric can be thought of as both simple and traditional. Its first 11 lines deal with a theme that is as old as English poetry – the coming of spring – in a way that would not have made the Georgian poets feel ill at ease. A precise but imaginative observer depicts a scene that is familiar to most readers in unrhymed, two-beat lines. The precision shows itself in the first line, with the use of the word "longer" to modify evenings, the accurate description of a fact, the lingering light of late winter or early spring. The imagination shows itself in the personification implied by the phrase "foreheads of houses." Both precision and imagination combine in the lines that conclude the first section of the poem:

> Its fresh-peeled voice
> Astonishing the brickwork.

The "serene foreheads of houses" are astonished by the singing of a thrush and the observer interprets the song, the source of the astonishment, "It will be spring soon."

This recognition of meaning causes the observer to look inward and describe his own reaction in terms that might have shocked the Georgian poets but help to explain the enthusiasm of critics and readers in post-war Britain:

> And I, whose childhood
> Is a forgotten boredom,
> Feel like a child
> Who comes on a scene
> Of adult reconciling,
> And can understand nothing
> But the unusual laughter
> And starts to be happy.

To describe childhood as "a forgotten boredom" is the kind of frankness that has a slightly comic effect. The elimination of child labour, Freud's emphasis on the importance of childhood for the shaping of adult personalities, and the sad consequences of two World

Wars had made something of a cult of childhood. Larkin's brief, clear, and personal statement is at once shocking, true, and funny, because deflationary.

Years later, interviewers could not refrain from asking Larkin, "Was your childhood really 'a forgotten boredom?'" – as if holding such a view were a sin or a crime. But what these interviewers failed to notice was that Larkin in the poem goes on to give a precise rendering of a childhood experience, a lingering memory of a childhood experience, an experience dependent on "adult re-conciling" that brings about "unusual laughter" and the beginning of a happiness that the child could not understand. This little scene, whether based on memory or observation, is an accurate and imaginative description of the feeling we experience with the recognition that spring is coming. The two sections of the poem, divided by the meaning assigned to the song of the thrush, are firmly but indirectly tied together, by implication. The forgotten boredom of winter has been astonished into a memory of ununderstandable happiness – spring. Figuratively speaking, the poem on the page is an equivalent of the song of the thrush, an uncalled-for piece of work by a "fresh-peeled voice" that astonishes the serene reader into memories of happiness that are like the first stirrings of spring yet cannot be fully understood or explained away.

It is this union of form and content, of what is said and the way it is said, that allows Larkin's work to give readers pleasure while standing up to re-readings and even critical scrutiny. I described the poem as unrhymed, for instance. But on closer examination occasional rhymes that support the fullest meaning of the poem can be found – "scene" linking up with "serene" to suggest a comparison of the adults with the houses. It could be argued that 'Coming' deals with poetic inspiration as much as with either spring or happiness. In fact, it deals with all three and in a way that simultaneously insists on their similarities, their differences, and their mystery, that is, our inability to understand them fully, even in maturity. The only response to them is gratitude. And it was gratitude that readers and critics felt for Larkin's work.

II

'Coming' is a good introduction to Larkin's poetry because it is not generally thought to be either one of his best or one of his best-known poems. In an interesting letter to the American poet Donald Hall, written in June, 1956, (that is, only eight months after the publication of *The Less Deceived* by the Marvell Press in Hessle, a Yorkshire village near Hull), Larkin advised Hall on selecting poems by Larkin for publication in an anthology this way:

> My feeling is that you would probably do best to pick poems that appeal to you, since you are nearer the readers who will buy the anthology, but the most-liked pieces are, in no sort of order, Church Going, Lines On A Young Lady's Photograph Album, Deceptions, I Remember, Poetry of Departures, At Grass, and Arrivals, Departures. I like all these and in addition have special affection for Absences (read 'sea' for 'floor' in line 1), Age, Latest Face, If My Darling, and Coming.

This letter is of interest for a number of reasons. First, it shows how rapidly Larkin's reputation grew on both sides of the Atlantic following the publication of *The Less Deceived.* Second, it shows how early Larkin equated the value of a poem with its 'appeal' for a reader – insisting on pleasure and attraction as the crux of the relationship between poem and reader, rather than significance, or importance, or the meaningfulness of the content of the poem. Third, the result of this relationship between a poem and its readers can well be that some of the poet's favourite poems do not attract or please many readers. Fourth, the letter shows that Philip Larkin, like authors before and since him, suffered from the curse of a printed error in his book. And, finally, the letter is of interest because it never mentions one of Larkin's best-known poems from *The Less Deceived* as either a popular favourite or a favourite of the author – 'Toads.' 'Toads', along with 'Church Going' and 'At Grass', have become generally accepted as the three indispensable Larkin poems from *The Less Deceived,* not only good poems but poems that seem to speak for their time, to make articulate what others half-consciously thought or felt in silence. It was this ability to perform a public function, to speak for the age, combined with the praise of critics and the enthusiasm of readers, that marked Larkin out as someone special, as potentially that rare thing in the twentieth century, a popular poet.

All three of these poems deal with big issues – religion in the case of 'Church Going', work in the case of 'Toads', and fame and death in the case of 'At Grass' – but in an idiosyncratic way, a way that came to be known as 'Larkinesque.' This idiosyncratic approach came about in part, at least, because of the point of view of the speaker of these poems, an identifiable character or persona that eventually merged in the public mind with Philip Larkin, the librarian at the University of Hull. This persona was most fully elaborated in 'Church Going', what probably remains Larkin's best-known poem. 'Church Going' is the longest poem in *The Less Deceived* and the centrepiece of the book, the 15th poem in a collection of 29 poems. It is easy to see why readers and critics alike immediately responded to the poem. It is a magnificent and impressive structure itself, like a church, but built of ten-line stanzas of rhyming or near-rhyming iambic pentameter. Its form harks back to the grandeur of poetry's past while remaining distinctively new and contemporary. It begins as a personal poem that does not state or argue for a point of view but rather describes a change of heart so that it ends as a public poem. Literally nothing happens in the poem after the first two stanzas but a record of thought and feeling. Ringing the changes on the point of view of the poem's speaker or persona gives the poem its form and its content.

Some commentators later angered Larkin by claiming that 'Church Going' was a religious poem. Both the poet and the commentators were right. The poem is not and should not be read as a religious poem in the sense that it accepts traditional religious beliefs. But the poem is not an agnostic poem, either, in the sense that traditional religious beliefs are simply old hat and laughable. The poem starts with mockery and moves to seriousness – the alteration, if not the conversion, in the literal sense of a 'turning away', that the speaker of the poem undergoes. The mocking attitude of the speaker concludes with the final lines of the second stanza, "I sign the book, donate an Irish sixpence, /Reflect the place was not worth stopping for." At this point the poem would have ended if it had been composed by a simple-minded and certain agnostic or atheist. Larkin had the honesty to pursue his own thoughts and feelings beyond 'isms', beyond any institutionalised thoughts, whether religious or anti-religious. Instead he lets his feelings and thoughts lead him where they would. In this poem, they led him to feel "at a loss" and this sense causes him to wonder. He wonders out loud about the future of churches – aware that belief is gone, he considers them as potential museums, or the vacant and forgotten haunts of the superstitious, only to finally ask, "And what remains when disbelief has gone?" This question provokes the speaker to think about a time when the last person will seek out the church and its grounds for what they were. He imagines as one possibility his "representative", someone who is "bored, uninformed" but drawn to the place "because it held unspilt/So long and equably what since is found/Only in separation – marriage, and birth,/And death, and thoughts of these." With this recognition, comes the realisation of why the speaker stopped at the church in the first place, "It pleases me to stand in silence here." Pleasure is the justification of the paradox of stopping at a place that does not intellectually seem worth stopping for. With this realisation, the speaker pronounces the last stanza, a stanza that shifts again in tone because it is pronounced with hard-won knowledge and the assurance that affords. The voice becomes public because it speaks for a community, referring to "all our compulsions", not just the thoughts or feelings of an individual, the 'I' of the poem. From this public position, the speaker declares the answer to all the questions raised in the poem – about the future uses of church buildings and what remains when disbelief is gone. The speaker asserts that he has discovered what "never can be obsolete", that is, "someone will forever be surprising/A hunger in himself to be more serious."

It is hard to resist the notion that 'Church Going' is a metaphor for poetry reading or writing. The magnificent structure of the poem would have been a fragmented failure if it ended with the second stanza, the mocking conclusion the place was not worth stopping for, the attitude of prose. Reading or writing poetry is equivalent to the pleasure that comes of standing in silence, ruminating, thinking, and feeling. But these silent activities lead to a kind of knowledge, a kind of knowledge that cannot be demonstrated scientifically or proven mathematically. It can only be asserted by the poet and believed or disbelieved by readers. This kind of knowledge often rests on a paradox. The hunger to be more serious comes as a surprise, to the poet and the reader alike. This surprise is equivalent to the "astonishing" voice of the thrush in 'Coming'. It suggests that we are not as we think we are, that we are other than we think we are, and it is this shared secret awareness that forms a community between poets and readers, a community based on common mysteries, "marriage, and birth,/And death, and thoughts of these." Just as the speaker of 'Coming' asserts that his childhood was "a forgotten boredom" and proceeds to give evidence of its memorability and even occasional happiness, so the speaker of 'Church Going' insists that his representative will be bored and uninformed while demonstrating in the words of the poem their opposites – eager attention to detail and a wealth of knowledge. If there is a 'Larkinesque' persona, it can perhaps be best defined by this need to strike a pose while undermining the pose's validity. Larkin perhaps unintentionally described the nature of his poems in a line from one of the poems for which he had great affection, 'If, My Darling' – "Each one double-yolked with meaning and meaning's rebuttal."

The Larkinesque persona is even more in evidence in 'Toads'. It is here fully developed as a tone of voice, a confiding conversational speaking voice that again changes its point of view while it has its say but with less reliance on objects or props than is the case in 'Church Going'. The voice establishes itself and its subject in the very first stanza:

> Why should I let the toad *work*
> Squat on my life?
> Can't I use my wit as a pitchfork
> And drive the brute off?

The remaining eight stanzas of the poem answer these questions. The poem continues to use the contractions and near-rhymes of the first stanza but nonetheless undergoes a number of shifts in tone. These shifts divide the poem into four sections that establish a logical sequence: the first two stanzas state the problem; stanzas three to five consider the experiences of others; stanzas six to eight draw the speaker's conclusions; and the final stanza serves as a summation. What marks the tone of voice is that it is at once self-critical, funny, and sad. The comic sense is most pronounced in stanza three, perhaps, where alliteration is used to heighten the effect of a comic list or catalogue:

> Lots of folk live on their wits:
> Lecturers, lispers,
> Losels, loblolly-men, louts –
> They don't end as paupers.

The list is comic not only because of the alliteration – used on a smaller scale in 'Church Going' in the line "Their parchment, plate and pyx in locked cases," – but also because of a kind of creative redundancy. Losels and loblolly-men are kinds of louts. Losels are worthless persons and loblolly is a mess of gruel but was also a dialect equivalent of lout. But the comedy and self-criticism combine in the sixth stanza. The speaker concludes that no matter what "lots of folk" do, he is not able to drive the "toad *work*" from his life. He states this conclusion in language that verges on the coarse while producing one of the most famous puns in 20th century poetry, a pun based on a line from a famous speech in *The Tempest* by Shakespeare, "We are such stuff as dreams are made on,/And our little life is rounded with a sleep." Larkin's stanza reads:

> Ah, were I courageous enough
> To shout *Stuff your pension*!
> But I know, all too well, that's the stuff
> That dreams are made on:

With this passage the tone shifts dramatically and becomes confessional, admitting that the speaker's adversary is not only the "toad *work*" but also another, inner something:

> For something sufficiently toad-like
> Squats in me, too;
> Its hunkers are heavy as hard luck,
> And cold as snow,
>
> And will never allow me to blarney
> My way to getting
> The fame and the girl and the money
> All at one sitting.

I don't say, one bodies the other
    One's spiritual truth;
But I do say it's hard to lose either,
    When you have both.

What is this "something sufficiently toad-like" that squats in the speaker? He does not directly say. It is a state of mind, rather than an activity like work. Coming after the reference to courage in the preceding stanza, it might be cowardice. But the description of this toad-like something does not seem to fit cowardice precisely – it is heavy and cold and prevents the speaker from getting out of life what popular films and novels perhaps lead us to expect from it, "The fame and the girl and the money/All at one sitting", as if they were the winnings to be gathered in at the end of a successful game of cards. On the other hand, the toad-like something is not merely a love of comfort and unrisky respectability, a possible internal equivalent of work. That identification is denied by the concluding stanza, the summary that is willing to generalise. It is perhaps just as well that the poem does not name this toad-like something and leaves each reader free to take it for any and all inhibitors to a full life. Still, it seems likely that the something is a fear of death – heavy, cold, coming on the heels of an allusion to one of Shakespeare's considerations of the end of life and leading to Larkin's consideration of "spiritual truth." It is at least this suggestion of the fear of death, squatting in the speaker, that gives the poem's concluding lines their clear-eyed inevitability and their sadness, a touch of pathos that refrains from self-pity because it sums up a condition common to the bulk of humanity. After all, if Larkin's life is not like that of the hero of a popular film or novel, neither is that of his readers.

This insistence on the unheroic or anti-heroic is another characteristic of the Larkinesque persona. But Larkin never or but rarely wallows in the unheroic. He is driven to this outlook by honesty but admits regrets. There can be little doubt that he would have liked to have had the courage to shout "*Stuff your pension*!" and blarney his way to getting the fame and the girl and the money. But he did not and could not – just as most of us do not and can not. To be able to make a memorable poem from that realisation was perhaps a consolation for him and for us.

An interviewer whose approach to poetry irritated Larkin a good deal asked him to comment on a critic's statement that Larkin's "favourite subjects" are "failure and weakness." Larkin said:

> I think a poet should be judged by what he does with his subjects, not by what his subjects are. Otherwise you're getting near the totalitarian attitude of wanting poems about steel production figures .... Poetry isn't a kind of paint-spray you use to cover selected subjects. A good poem about failure is a success.

He could have been thinking about 'Toads'.

III

'At Grass' is the final poem in *The Less Deceived.* The first person singular, the 'I' of the Larkinesque persona, disappears and becomes instead an "eye" in the poem's first line, "The eye can hardly pick them out". The "them" of that first line does not refer to people but to two ageing racehorses. The disappearance of the first person singular and the concentration on non-human subjects give the poem a stately objectivity, almost as if life is viewed in the poem from the unhurried and unemotional perspective of the dead. This stateliness is mirrored in the poem's form. It consists of five six-line stanzas of iambic tetrameter rhymed a, b, c, a, b, c. There are no contractions in this poem and its rhymes are primarily full rather than near rhymes. The language has neither the jokey, confiding quality of that in 'Toads' nor the exalted quality of the conclusion of 'Church Going.' The language of this poem is closest to the precise but imaginative description of the first section of 'Coming.'

Larkin prided himself on the idea that his poems required no commentators, critics, or interpreters. By and large, he felt they contained no references to ancient myths, exotic religions, or out-of-the-way learning that required elucidation, no allusions to other poems that the average educated reader would be unaware of, and no language that is unnecessarily or intentionally obscure. He argued that the motive behind the writing of a poem (to the extent that it could be known) was to preserve – to preserve a scene or a feeling or an experience in words that would allow readers to see or sense or share what the poet had experienced. 'At Grass' is such a poem.

There is no need to comment on it. The only thing to do with a poem like this one is to read and re-read it. It says all there is to be said about it. And that is the highest praise that can be offered on its behalf.

IV

The Less Deceived seemed to come fully developed out of nowhere. That was a false impression that no doubt added to the success of the book and helped to spread Larkin's reputation. The poems in the collection also seemed to have an unliterary or anti-literary quality – if literariness is associated with a false pretentiousness, a strained use of language intended to convince readers that the poet is more learned, or sexy, or exciting, or given to extraordinary feelings and experiences than he actually is. This unliterary quality has nothing to do with illiteracy. The poems in the collection are of a consistently high quality but more importantly display a surprising and unexpected diversity. Larkin uses a wide range of verse forms and rhetorical devices with extraordinary skill, the kind of artlessness that conceals an unusual dedication to his poetry, an offhandedness that takes technique and form for granted.

The 'unliterary' is often thought of as springing directly from life rather than from other works of literature. But even the four poems from the collection considered here show connections to the works of others. The thrush in 'Coming' is likely to owe something to 'The Darkling Thrush' by Thomas Hardy, a poet Larkin admired and acknowledged a deep indebtedness to. The church in 'Church Going' is likely to owe something to the temple in Norman Cameron's 'The Disused Temple', a poem Larkin chose to include in his anthology, *The Oxford Book of Twentieth Century English Verse* (1973). The use of a quotation from Shakespeare is crucial to the success of 'Toads'. And while I am unaware of any overt allusions to other poems in 'At Grass', it clearly stands in a tradition that runs back through Edward Thomas and A.E. Housman to one of the major strands of poetry in English.

The next chapter will deal with Larkin's long and demanding apprenticeship, a series of false starts from which he eventually emerged with the publication of *The Less Deceived* at the age of 33.

2 The Apprenticeship

The length and arduousness of Larkin's apprenticeship can best be grasped by considering the books he published before *The Less Deceived* appeared in 1955. But a poet's apprenticeship is not restricted to technique, to the use of words. The emotional development that is an integral part of a poet's apprenticeship can be traced in Larkin's case by considering the people to whom he dedicated his early books. Those dedications describe a trajectory from Larkin's family, through male friendship and companionship, to a woman from outside Larkin's family circle. They also describe a trajectory from ambition, through apparent failure, to a rueful acceptance of limitations. Although it will be necessary to discuss these aspects of the apprenticeship separately, they took place simultaneously and are clearly, if implicitly, bound together.

I

One clear sign of Larkin's precocity and youthful ambition is 'Ultimatum', a poem he wrote when he was only 17 years old. The poem was published in *The Listener* after his 18th birthday when he was in his first year as an undergraduate at St John's College, Oxford, about a year after the outbreak of World War II in September 1939. It is less the technical quality of this poem (it is a skilfully and idiosyncratically contrived sonnet that shows the youthful poet was already at home with the use of assonance or near rhymes and includes lines that at least hint at the mature Larkin ["For any term of time beyond the years", for instance)] than the fact that it is so imitative of Auden, so derivative, that it gives off the impression of a practice exercise rather than something that the poet has an urgent need to say. It is literary, in the worst sense, as the work of the mature Larkin was not.

In later life, Larkin freely admitted that as a schoolboy Auden seemed to him to be the only available alternative to "old-fashioned poetry". That 'Ultimatum' was published suggests the extent to which imitations of Auden were considered acceptable by editors, a style of the period rather than of an individual. But the relative silence of

Larkin following this publication is a clear sign of his integrity, an inner check on his ambition. He certainly could have followed this poem up by publishing more imitations – he wrote many. Instead, he periodically published some early poems in undergraduate magazines or kept his apprentice work to himself. Despite the derivative nature of 'Ultimatum', it is worth taking note of one of its statements – "Exploded the ancient saying: Life is yours". This line briefly articulates a widespread outlook of the youth of the time. The bombings of World War II made the future a question mark – the personal future as well as the public future of everyone "on our island". That fact shaped the outlook of an entire generation – Larkin's generation. By the time this poem appeared, Auden himself had left England for the United States – putting an end to the Auden generation and perhaps inspiring the youthful Larkin to consider the "need for emigration". Years later, when Larkin wrote book reviews, he argued that Auden's best work was finished when he left England because that work was connected to a specific time and place, that social conditions had been one source of its power and the excitement it produced in young readers.

From boyhood upwards, Larkin wrote poetry and prose almost constantly. He wrote short stories as well as poems and kept diaries that contained both prose and verse. Although he would later claim that he wanted to be a novelist rather than a poet, at the end of each year he went through the poems he had written, selected those he liked the best, made them into little books, and wrote critical comments about them and preserved them. This youthful practice again shows his ambition – it suggests that the undergraduate had one eye on posterity and a conviction that the future would take an interest in what he wrote – but also shows a growing critical sense, an ability to detect the sources and shortcomings of what he wrote. One admirable aspect of the mature Larkin was his own sure sense of the quality of his own poems and the severity with which he considered them before publishing them much less collecting them in a book.

If he published little as an undergraduate, that little was enough for him to gain some reputation at the university as a writer of poetry. It was this reputation that led to the publication of his first book, *The North Ship*, a full decade before *The Less Deceived* appeared. There is no need to go through the contents of that first book in detail.

Larkin's own description of its contents is enough to indicate the part the book played in his apprenticeship:

> Looking back, I find in the poems not one abandoned self but several – the ex-schoolboy, for whom Auden was the only alternative to 'old-fashioned' poetry; the undergraduate, whose work a friend affably characterised as 'Dylan Thomas, but you've a sentimentality that's all your own'; and the immediately post-Oxford self, isolated in Shropshire with a complete Yeats stolen from the local girls' school.

While this comment is fair enough in general terms, there are themes and lines in *The North Ship* that do suggest the mature Larkin and some of the characteristic traits of his work. The eye for realistic details in these lines and the implied setting in which they are spoken provide an example:

> I lie and wait for morning, and the birds,
> The first steps going down the unswept street,
> Voices of girls with scarves around their heads.

The distinctive rhythm of these iambic pentameter lines – as much as their content – help to bring to mind such a late poem as 'Aubade'.

Larkin's work had appeared in an anthology, *Poetry From Oxford in Wartime*, published by a small publishing house, the Fortune Press. The proprietor of the press wrote inviting Larkin to submit a collection of poems for publication. He typed up the contents of *The North Ship* and the book appeared in July, 1945, months after the end of hostilities in Europe and just before World War II ended following the dropping of atomic bombs on Japanese cities, acts that could have seemed to give the words "Exploded the ancient saying: Life is yours" a global application.

The "immediately post-Oxford self" was the self who wanted to be a novelist. If 'Ultimatum' suggests Larkin's precocity in the skilful use of words, it is as nothing when compared to *Jill* and *A Girl in Winter*, the novels he wrote and published soon after leaving Oxford. Both are good novels but it is unlikely that either would be remembered now if they had not been written by Philip Larkin. They are the kinds of books that would have quietly fallen into oblivion only to have someone stumble over them occasionally and become enthusiastic about them. Both of them are capable of arousing enthusiasm in readers.

Jill, written during the war, when Larkin was living at home with his parents while looking for work and then at Wellington in Shropshire where he first became a librarian, has been credited with an historical interest, apart from whatever merits it has as a novel. It has been described as containing "the first example of that characteristic landmark of the British post-war novel, the displaced working-class hero". Larkin argued that while this sounded true enough, it was a coincidental or accidental matter. John Kemp, the anti-hero of *Jill*, certainly has a working-class background, but his class is used in the book to provide him with a handicap, a way to make him socially ill at ease and cut off. There is no denunciation of the class system in the book and it is not at all a left-wing exposé or anything like that. Kemp's class is no doubt, as Larkin suggested, an equivalent of Larkin's stammer – one of the things that cut him off from his contemporaries and made him socially ill at ease. What is important about *Jill* from the point of view of Larkin's apprenticeship is his ability to tell a realistic story. It is a briskly-paced narrative, with comic elements like those that would later appear in some of Larkin's verse, that displays a remarkable ear for dialogue, Larkin's ability to speak in a number of voices and shift those voices rapidly. When it is remembered that the novel was largely written when Larkin was 21 years old, *Jill* constitutes a remarkable tour de force.

A Girl in Winter, again set and mostly written during the war when Larkin was a librarian at Wellington, is a very different kind of novel. The protagonist is a young woman, Katherine Lind, from an unspecified country, working in a library in England during the war. While the book contains touches of realism, it aspires to a symbolistic style. It is slower-paced than *Jill* and its meaning is less readily apparent, suggested more than stated. In bald terms, the author seems to be more interested in form than in content, more interested in producing a work of art than in telling a story, and there is a slightly precious aspect to the result, an attempt to manipulate the substance in a way that gives the novel a contrived, carefully-written feel. Larkin later said that he had been excited by articles in *Scrutiny*, the critical journal, on the possibilities of the novel as a dramatic poem. This interest in theory gives the novel something in common with Larkin's early verse, a static ambiguity that is well crafted but potentially baffling or at least unrewarding for readers. The novels of Virginia Woolf perhaps did to this novel what Yeats's poems did to Larkin's early verse. Despite all that, the book remains highly readable and again represents something of a tour de force that can leave no doubt about the dedication, time, thought, and effort Larkin devoted to working at becoming a writer.

Jill, like *The North Ship*, was published by the Fortune Press and brought its author neither payment nor public recognition. *A Girl in Winter*, on the other hand, was published by the highly respected house of Faber & Faber, in 1947. The book sold 5,000 copies and some reviewers spotted in it an impressive talent with real promise. Some reviewers expressed high hopes for the young novelist's next book. By the age of 25, Larkin had moved from Wellington to become an Assistant Librarian at University College, Leicester, and had every reason to believe that his career as a novelist was properly launched. His publishers were anxious for the manuscript of his next novel and he set to work on it immediately. But a strange thing happened. He found that he could not write another novel that satisfied him. Worse, he prepared a manuscript for another collection of poems only to have it rejected by numerous publishers.

In 1950, he took a job as Sub-Librarian at Queen's University, Belfast. It might have seemed to him that librarianship, something he had taken up almost by accident until his dream of being a novelist came true, had become his only real career. But in Belfast he wrote many of the poems that were collected in *The Less Deceived*. There he established a way of life that would last for years. He was to be a poet and a librarian, not a novelist as he had hoped after all.

II

The infant Larkin, showing a hesitation in the face of change like that he would display throughout his life, was reluctant to be born. He arrived a month late, on a night with a full moon, 9th August 1922, in Coventry. The extra month in the womb made him a large baby, weighing nearly ten pounds, and with a full head of longish black hair.

He was christened Philip Arthur Larkin, a compromise reached by his parents. His father wanted to name him Philip Sydney Larkin, after the Elizabethan poet, soldier, and courtier. His mother held out for Arthur as the newborn's middle name as a way to honour her brother. This compromise over the child's name seems to mirror the diverse outlooks of his parents – the father with a public, historical, and literary sense and the mother concentrating on the present and the family. The uneasy union of these diverse outlooks gave Larkin the gift of life but also placed him in an idiosyncratic, tension-filled home, the kind of place that led him to describe his childhood as "unspent" and "a forgotten boredom", at least when he compared it with the recorded childhoods of his literary heroes.

Larkin's father, himself named Sydney, seems to have been a dominant personality as well as something of a public figure. In Larkin's childhood he was City Treasurer of Coventry, a growing industrial town known for its cathedral and as a centre of automobile manufacturing. Sydney earned a reputation as an able administrator, as a clear, forceful thinker who could express himself well in speech and writing, and as an outspoken holder of slightly eccentric opinions. The timing of Larkin's birth had been dictated by the progress of Sydney's career. Larkin's sister, Catherine, had been born early in the marriage but Sydney decided that they should not have a second child until he was fully prepared financially to do so. This kind of family planning seems to have been typical of Sydney Larkin's rationalism.

Larkin's mother, Eva Emily Day Larkin, on the other hand, was a nervous and retiring soul. She was made all but hysterical by thunderstorms, tired easily, and seemed incompetent to deal with running a household. She had early considered librarianship as a profession but had instead briefly become a teacher.

The meeting and courtship of Larkin's parents reads like pages of a novel by Thomas Hardy – a writer who was certainly admired by both the father and the son and perhaps by the mother and sister as well. (Sydney Larkin delivered a paper on Hardy before a local society in Coventry that met to encourage the literary and philosophical interests of its members.) Larkin's parents met in 1906 when Sydney was cycling on the Welsh coast at a seaside resort where Eva was on holiday with her family. They separately sought shelter in the same spot from a rainstorm. Sydney was impressed when Eva responded to his attempts to make her acquaintance by reading a book. They were both bookish people. At the end of a three-day acquaintanceship, they were engaged to be married, a testimony to Sydney's decisiveness and persistence. They corresponded and enjoyed occasional visits for five years until Sydney was in a position to marry, in 1911. He qualified as an accountant and became active in professional societies, specialising in the financial management of cities.

When Larkin was a boy, his family lived in a substantial house in the centre of Coventry and his mother was assisted in running the house by the services of a series of maids. There is little question that the family could have afforded to send him to a public school. But Sydney Larkin, no doubt seeing himself as a 'self-made man', felt an animosity towards the public school system and the élitism it fostered. Larkin went to the King Henry VIII school in Coventry from the age of eight until he was nearly 18, living at home the entire time.

Perhaps too much has been made of the idiosyncrasies of Larkin's parents and the unhappiness of his childhood. He was certainly raised in comfortable circumstances by parents who were both fond and proud of him. He was provided with electric trains to play with, was encouraged to read, and when he later developed a love for jazz, his parents provided him with a drum kit. The difficulty was that the family stayed to themselves – with no friends or relatives streaming through to relieve the vaguely tense and sad atmosphere that permeated the home. Schoolboy friends remembered the house as well-kept but quiet and unwelcoming. Larkin's recollection was that his father worked all day and either closeted himself to read or gardened in the evenings. Perhaps his clearest, if ambivalent, statement on his parents was: "Probably both my parents were rather shy people – of each other, of their children ... I wouldn't want it thought that I didn't like my parents. I did like them. But at the same time they were rather awkward people and not very good at being happy. And these things rub off".

He not only liked his parents but loved them. But he also tended to blame them, privately and publicly, for his own awkwardness and unhappiness – a sign of his own lingering immaturity. It was no doubt this private and public stance that led Andrew Motion, in his lengthy, official biography of Larkin, to make so much of Sydney's admiration of and enthusiasm for Hitler's Germany, with the result that some commentators have tried to portray both father and son as crypto-Nazis – a result that is unfair to both of them and misleading. The period between the wars was a highly political, chaotic time, tinged by antagonism to capitalism – the economic system that had led to the catastrophic fratricidal watershed of World War I. Sydney Larkin was an admirer of not only Thomas Hardy but also H.G. Wells, D.H. Lawrence, and George Bernard Shaw. His intellectual and professional interests no doubt led him to a kind of socialism, the Fabianism of Shaw as expounded in Shaw's *An Intelligent Woman's Guide to Socialism.*

Like Shaw and many other thinkers who lost their religious faith, Sydney Larkin made something of a god of the State – a god he served and flourished under as a priestly accountant. This kind of socialism had nothing in common with either the utopian socialism Oscar Wilde called for in his *The Soul of Man Under Socialism* or the revolutionary communism of Marx, with its emphasis on class struggle. It was instead evolutionary, gradual, rational and efficient, and appealed to a broad audience of intellectuals, office workers, and government employees. Its aim was not the abolition of the State but the nationalisation of industries. Nazi, it must be remembered, was short for National Socialist. It was not unusual for someone like Sydney Larkin to find his political ideals being put into practice in Hitler's Germany. Shaw admired both Stalin and Mussolini.

Dictators with socialist rhetoric fooled many people with better minds than that of Sydney Larkin into becoming admirers and adherents. If he had been an admirer of Stalin, who after allying himself with Hitler became the ally of England against Germany, it would probably pass with little or no comment. What was unusual about him was that he publicly flaunted his admiration for Hitler while holding a public office. He also seems to have taken a sardonic glee in predicting a German victory in the early stages of World War II. This was no doubt part of a public pose, a protective mask for a man who was at root timid and arrogant or, as his son said, shy. His political position was more pathetic than sinister.

Larkin's own right-wing views were more cultural than political. As he told an interviewer: "I've always been right-wing. It's difficult to say why, but not being a political thinker I suppose I identify the

Right with certain virtues and the Left with certain vices. All very unfair, no doubt". He went on to list the virtues of the Right as "thrift, hard work, reverence, and desire to preserve." He gave the vices he identified with the Left as "idleness, greed and treason". Like his father, he enjoyed striking a public pose that might provoke people into thought, but in his personal relations he is reported to have been polite, kind, and considerate even to those who, based on his opinions, should have seemed to him intolerable. These attitudes grew directly from his boyhood and early experiences. School at first seems to have been a kind of torture for him. He developed a severe stammer at the age of four. It would be interesting to know the circumstances under which the stammer came about. It is likely that his tendency to be honest and outspoken provoked one or the other of his parents or his sister (or perhaps all three) causing him to become self-conscious and unsure of himself when he spoke. He was also extremely short-sighted, a condition that went undetected and uncorrected for years. The result was that he sat in class unsure of what was written on the board and fearful that he would be called upon to say something. Eventually, he was fitted with specs and made some good friends among his schoolmates, particularly James Ballard Sutton, Colin Gunner, and Noel Hughes.

These boys soon discovered that Larkin had a strong sense of humour and a gift for mimicry. The masters at the school remembered him as an exceedingly polite, almost courtly boy. His friends remembered him for the wicked sarcasm and mockery he aimed at the masters after school. His earliest writings seem to have been records of his daily life, sometimes comic and sometimes sentimental. There is the sense that he did not seem fully to exist until he had set his life down on paper. He contributed verse and prose to *The Coventrian*, the magazine of the school. And he developed a life-long passion for American jazz, an emotional release that he shared with some schoolmates that put them at odds with the adult world of masters and parents.

Sydney Larkin seems to have been happy to pay his son's fees at Oxford and publicly displayed understandable pride when Philip took a First Class degree in English Language and Literature. Larkin's stay at the university seems to have begun by repeating his experience at school, his stammering left him socially awkward and ill at ease but he came to make good friends because of his humour, the love of jazz, and literary interests. The biggest change was that he lived away from home for the first time and had the chance to draw friends from a wider circle. He dressed like an aesthete – loud jackets, pink shirts, provocative bow ties – but behaved in a way that one of his undergraduate friends, Kingsley Amis, described as that of a "non-gamesplaying hearty". Larkin's memorable foul mouth, his drinking, smoking, belching, and farting, his comic sense, sarcasm, and mimicry, made him appear exceedingly tough and tough-minded.

He did not only continue to write at the university but also met there others who wished to write, and established poets and authors – George Orwell, Dylan Thomas, and Vernon Watkins. It was Watkins' admiration for Yeats that proved to be so irresistible for Larkin. When *The North Ship* was published, Larkin sent a copy to Watkins. But Larkin's undergraduate experience was unusual because of the war. Unlike most of his friends, he was found unfit for military service because of his poor eyesight. J.B. Sutton, the childhood friend who wanted to be a painter and who had gone to the Slade Art College which was then housed at the Ashmolean in Oxford, had to interrupt his training to enter the service. Kingsley Amis' academic career was also interrupted by service in the Signal Corps. Larkin left the university with few prospects for a career but with no need to worry about going into the armed forces. It was in this state of suspended animation that he began to write *Jill*.

One sign of the radical difference between the First and Second World Wars is the associations conjured up by place-names of each war. Flanders, the Somme, the Ardennes still call up the memory of massive pitched battles between armies during World War I. World War II produced a very different set of place-names. Auschwitz, Dachau, and Belsen are names darkened and bloodied not by pitched battles by combatants but by the systematic torture and murder of civilians – a bestiality of which beasts are incapable – stern reminders of the depravities humans can perform when the traditional checks and restraints are loosened or lost. Hiroshima and Nagasaki are darkened and bloodied not by pitched battles by combatants but by a long-range, technological destruction of largely civilian populations. The names of Dresden and Coventry still carry with them the memory of the saturation bombing of civilians. Because he was unfit for military service, Larkin experienced the war as a civilian and the bombing of Coventry taught him just how much he loved his family and feared for their safety. When he was unable to reach them, he and a friend left the university to search for their families. Larkin could not locate his or learn anything about them. Only after his return to Oxford did he learn that they were safe. Larkin's sense of panic still haunts the pages of *Jill*, in which this search of the bombed streets of his hometown is described.

Larkin's early poems and *Jill* focus attention on his difficulties with love and sex. The very vagueness of the early poems parallels the fantasy life of John Kemp, a fantasy life that leads him to a humiliating disaster. Larkin distanced himself from the anti-hero of his first novel and critics have tended to follow his lead. There is no question that Kemp is a fictional character, not an attempt at autobiography. But Kingsley Amis, who admired the novel, shrewdly noticed that there was a split in Larkin's youthful character to which Amis had remained oblivious until he read the book. Amis wrote:

> The experiences of the hero, John Kemp, in wartime Oxford were instantly attributable to the visible Philip; Kemp's fantasy life, dreamy, romantic, sensitive, seemed the work of a different person. I found them impossible to reconcile – well, so had the author. This set me pondering, and I have hardly finished doing so yet.

Amis meant by "the visible Philip" the "non-gamesplaying hearty". He wrote these words shortly after he received the news of Larkin's death. Larkin also pondered this split and its relationship to his sexual development much of the time. It seems clear that his school days were spent with his family and male friends, with no contact to speak of with girls. He seems to have had some romantic attachments to schoolmates with no sign of overt homosexuality. The fullest and funniest record of Larkin's apprenticeship appears in his letters to J.B. Sutton, letters that have now been published. In those letters it is clear that Larkin thought of Sutton as his closest and best friend but also as an artistic ally, a fellow devotee of the writings of D.H. Lawrence, and a fellow artist. He sometimes daydreamed of their going to the United States after the war or of their becoming famous simultaneously in England. He also wrote Sutton that he thought his awkwardness and difficulties with women arose from a 'mother fixation' and that the example of the unhappiness of his parents had soured his wish to marry and raise a family. There is evidence in Larkin's life and work that if he had a 'mother fixation' his attempts to overcome it were complicated by the presence in his family circle of his older sister, Catherine or Kitty.

Larkin became engaged to a young woman named Ruth Bowman when he was a librarian at Wellington. She was a 16 year old school girl when they met and, as Andrew Motion has pointed out, she looked remarkably like Philip Larkin. What Motion does not point out is that this attraction for a schoolgirl version of himself is paralleled in John Kemp's fantasy life. Kemp invents a sister for himself, Jill, and later turns her into a girlfriend. The name of this invented sister and beloved carries a suggestion of the nursery through its allusion to the nursery rhyme, 'Jack and Jill', the possible pet names of John Kemp and his fictional love. Larkin's sister remembered that, when her parents went out, she had to care for Philip and put him to bed when she was a schoolgirl before she could settle down to do her homework and that this was "rather difficult". Larkin's "mother fixation" could well have been complicated by his having a younger, second mother around the house in his sister.

Larkin recognised that his shifting about for a writing style "was merely one aspect of a general immaturity." It is to his credit that he applied what Kingsley Amis described as his sometimes "frightening honesty" to himself as well as to others. In *A Girl in Winter* his main character is given a name that is surprisingly close to that of his sister – Katherine Lind. That she is from another country helps to disguise the closeness of the names. Nonetheless, the vague, symbolic quality of the writing suggests that Larkin was dealing with matter that was bound up with "invisible Philip" – the personality he kept hidden from school friends and fellow undergraduates but released in his early writings, the poems in *The North Ship*, dedicated to his parents "in gratitude", *Jill*, dedicated to his schoolmate and confidant, James Ballard Sutton, and *A Girl in Winter*, dedicated to Bruce Montgomery, a fellow undergraduate at Oxford.

Years later, Larkin expressed the guess that Montgomery had served as a "creative stimulus" for him. Montgomery was an extravagant and talented figure in wartime Oxford, a throwback to an earlier period, the days of Evelyn Waugh's *Brideshead Revisited* perhaps.

He had written a book entitled *Romanticism and the World Crisis*, he was a composer as well as an accomplished organist, he had painted one of the pictures that hung on the walls in his rooms, and he took 10 days to write *The Case of the Gilded Fly*, a detective story he published under the name of Edmund Crispin. He drank heavily, used a walking stick as he made his rounds through Oxford, and displayed what Larkin called "depths of frivolity". For a time, he and Larkin were frequent companions, drinking and laughing together and at times getting up to the kind of antics that would have earned Larkin a reputation similar to that of Dylan Thomas if they had been performed in Soho rather than in Shropshire.

One of the things that led Larkin to apply for and accept the library job at Wellington was its proximity to Shrewsbury, where Montgomery was then teaching. As a result, Montgomery became a confidant and literary colleague for Larkin when he was courting Ruth Bowman and writing *A Girl in Winter*. The book went to Faber & Faber because Montgomery's literary agent agreed to take it on. Larkin courted Ruth Bowman and became engaged to her, but he seems to have never been wholehearted about the relationship and they never married. His indecisiveness did not stem exclusively from the example of his parents. He and Ruth came to realise that he was not cut out for marriage. There were good things about their relationship. His stammer, which was still severe in public, soon disappeared when they were alone together. They shared literary and other interests and had enjoyable times together. But there were also times when he had periods of black depression and he would either say nothing or produce such harsh outbursts that she was shocked and hurt. In addition, in the spring of 1947, shortly after the publication of *A Girl in Winter*, he met Monica Jones, a lecturer in English at University College, Leicester, where Larkin had taken a job as Assistant Librarian.

Larkin and Monica Jones had a good deal in common. As Andrew Motion wrote, "Like him, Monica was often facetious about the things she took most seriously, and tough on subjects which touched her deeply … Contemporaries remember her as someone whose shyness turned easily to scorn. She was scathing about merely fashionable views, prone to fits of gloomy inertia, passionate in defence of writers she admired (particularly Crabbe and Scott) … Her idiosyncrasies were reflected in the 'rather special' way she dressed … With her inability to suffer fools, her slightly pouting mouth, and her abrupt speech, she contended with the world in style."

What Motion does not say is that Jones' taste in literature matched that of the mature Larkin more than that of the aesthete who had written *A Girl in Winter*. He also does not say that she, like Ruth Bowman, looked something like Larkin. She was another sister-like figure, but slightly older than Larkin rather than a number of years younger, and independent-minded. They never married but maintained what Motion calls "the most important relationship of his life" until he died. They went out together, corresponded, spent their holidays together, and in the end cared for each other when they were ill. His indecisiveness about Ruth Bowman and Monica Jones seems to parallel his inability to complete another novel or write poems that were totally his own. These were continuing consequences of his lingering immaturity.

There is a good deal of talk among critics about a poet's need to 'find his own voice', as if it were something that existed but had been temporarily mislaid. The problem is instead to find simultaneously the subject of a poem and the words to express it – words with an inevitability about them that surprises the poet and keeps them fresh for readers. It was probably Larkin's familiarity with this problem that caused him to describe the voice of the thrush in 'Coming' as "fresh-peeled". Many students of Larkin's poetry argue that he first 'found his voice' or produced a breakthrough poem when he wrote 'Going', the earliest of his poems to be collected in *The Less Deceived*. It seems to me that this occasion took place instead when he wrote a poem that he never published or even tried to publish in his lifetime but carefully preserved. It was an untitled elegy for his father.

Sydney Larkin died on 26th March 1948. He was cremated five days later. After the service, Catherine Larkin, who was by then married and a mother herself, said to her brother, "We're nobody now: he did it all". On 4th April, he wrote the first unmistakable Larkin poem:

> An April Sunday bring the snow
> Making the blossom on the plum trees green,
> Not white. An hour or two, and it will go.
> Strange that I spend that hour moving between

Cupboard and cupboard, shifting the store
Of jam you made of fruit from these same trees:
Five loads – a hundred pounds or more –
More than enough for all next summer's teas,

Which now you will not sit and eat.
Behind the glass, under the cellophane,
Remains your final summer – sweet
And meaningless, and not to come again.

There is nothing vague or emptily sonorous about this. It speaks
directly from a personal experience by moving from an accurate
observation of nature, through a self-dramatisation of the poet
performing a routine chore, to a generalisation marked by clarity,
honesty, and the sadness of strong feeling. There are also metaphors
for the kinds of poems Larkin was to continue to write in it. The
glass and the cellophane are transparent substances designed to
preserve at least temporarily the sweet meaninglessness of living.
He achieved maturity as a person and a personal style as a poet
through his experiences of love and death as much as through any
purely technical search for a style.

Driven to a state of paralysis by the conflicting loyalties he felt
for his widowed mother, Ruth Bowman, and Monica Jones, he let
his career lead him to make a decisive move. He left Leicestershire
for Belfast, eventually gave up the ambition to become a novelist,
and settled down to write the poems that only he could write. As he
would later say, he did not choose poetry, poetry chose him. It was
appropriate that he dedicated *The Less Deceived* to Monica Jones.

3   *The Whitsun Weddings*

When Philip Larkin took the post of Librarian at University College, Hull, he was what he would primarily remain for the rest of his life – a bachelor simultaneously drawn to and repelled by marriage who proved to be an able academic administrator and a leading poet of his time. Maeve Brennan, a colleague and friend at the library, recalled his arrival this way:

> When Miss Agnes Cuming, the retiring University Librarian, introduced us to her replacement, Philip Larkin, in March 1955, we wondered how this tall, spare, diffident young man would get on with us and we with him. By contrast, his dress was rather flamboyant: corduroy trousers, bright pink shirt and navy and white spotted bow tie. Later we were even more taken aback by the patterned ties with colorful fruit and flower designs which he alternated with bow ties in those days, and his penchant for brightly coloured socks. Moreover, his intellectual appearance and pronounced stammer distanced him from us. We knew little about him except that he had come from Queen's University, Belfast, where he had been sub-librarian, was thirty-two years old and unmarried. We knew nothing about his poetic aspirations and even the appearance of *The Less Deceived*, seven months after his arrival, caused no more than a faint ripple in our totally ordinary lives which were dominated by our boy friends, engagements and wedding plans, or their failure to come to fruition.

If Larkin's arrival was marked by awkwardness and a sense of distance, as in the past, his humour, interests, and compassion soon led him to become a friend and companion of many of the people on the library staff. He liked teasing the young women about their boyfriends and engagements and eagerly, if jokingly, expressed the hope for news of broken engagements – as his own had been some years before. But when such breakups actually occurred, the staff "discovered soon enough that his sympathy was genuine ..."

Larkin's career at the University was a busy one, in part because of the post-war boom in education and in part because he was able to see to it that the Library at Hull was very much a part of this boom. He described it to an interviewer in these terms:

> My job as University Librarian is a full-time one, five days a week, forty-five weeks a year. When I came to Hull, I had eleven staff; now there are over a hundred of one sort and another. We built one new library in 1960 and another in 1970, so that my first fifteen years were busy. Of course, this was a period of university expansion in England, and Hull grew as much as, if not more than, the rest.

As this statement and the comments of Maeve Brennan suggest, Larkin tried to keep his public career as a librarian separate from his private passion for poetry. He in fact expressed concern that the proximity of the Marvell Press to Hull would entangle the two. Instead, he succeeded fairly well in keeping these two aspects of his life separate until *The Whitsun Weddings* was published in 1964 and was awarded the Queen's Gold Medal for Poetry. After that, despite his refusal to give public readings and his initial reluctance to give interviews, he became something of a public figure as a poet.

Just as his career as a librarian was supported by the post-war expansion in education, his reputation as a poet was supported by a shift in literary taste. George Hartley, the proprietor of the Marvell Press, put it this way: "My poetry magazine *Listen*, 1954 to 1962, was fortunate enough, like Grigson's *New Verse*, to appear at a time when a new spirit was appearing in English poetry and early enough to promote the work of an emerging major poet." This comparison is an accurate one. New Verse had been founded as a platform for the young Auden and helped to establish a period style, a style that came to be known as 'Audenesque'. *Listen* served as a comparable platform for Larkin. But it was far from being the only one. BBC broadcasts by John Wain and others, anthologies prepared by D.J. Enright and Robert Conquest, and publication in a number of magazines all produced the look of Larkin being a part of a literary movement. In fact, it came to be called 'The Movement'.

There is no need to take up the history of 'The Movement' or join the debate over whether it ever actually existed, other than as a publicity campaign, at all. The important thing is that although Larkin appears to be an isolated figure, working all day as a librarian at

Hull, he in fact had literary friends, admirers, and allies who helped to establish his reputation and an audience for his work. Perhaps the funniest novel of the period, Kingsley Amis' *Lucky Jim*, published in 1954, was dedicated to Larkin, benefited from Larkin's suggestions and criticisms, and is based in part on Larkin's life at Leicester. The popularity of *Lucky Jim* in a way foreshadows the popularity and affection later felt for Larkin's work and his public persona. This development of an actual rather than an imagined audience no doubt helped to shape Larkin's thinking about poetry and the poems he wrote. One of the most drastic shifts in literature following the war was the willingness of writers to renew contact with that mythical creature, the common reader. Between the wars, poets and other writers seemed to turn their backs on common readers and to fence their work with 'No Trespassing' signs. Larkin expressed this new or renewed outlook on the relationship between poet and reader in a brief article called 'The Pleasure Principle', a title drawn from Freud:

> It is sometimes useful to remind ourselves of the simpler aspects of things normally regarded as complicated. Take, for instance, the writing of a poem. It consists of three stages: the first is when a man becomes obsessed with an emotional concept to such a degree that he is compelled to do something about it. What he does is the second stage, namely, construct a verbal device that will reproduce this emotional concept in anyone who cares to read it, anywhere, anytime. The third stage is the recurrent situation of people in different times and places setting off the device and re-creating in themselves what the poet felt when he wrote it. The stages are interdependent and all necessary. If there has been no preliminary feeling, the device has nothing to reproduce and the reader will experience nothing. If the second stage has not been well done, the device will not deliver the goods, or will deliver only a few goods to a few people, or will stop delivering them after an absurdly short while. And if there is no third stage, no successful reading, the poem can hardly be said to exist in a practical sense at all.

This statement makes clear Larkin's view of poetry when he was writing the poems that were eventually gathered in *The Whitsun Weddings*. It is interesting on a number of counts. It is a rational discussion of the irrational in terms that combine the scientific or technological with common sense. An obsession leads to a need to act and the action called for is the "construction" of "a verbal device" that will deliver the goods – the 'goods' being the cause of the obsession. What is described is a way to make the irrational seem rational, to make the private fit to appear in public. It is an ancient view of poetry, demanding both inspiration and technical skill, while holding the poet responsible for the quality of the poem and making "anyone who cares to read it, anywhere, any time" the sole judge of the poem. The thick jungle of criticism that sprang up to mediate between poems and readers in this century is effectively cut back by this view. Larkin did not only turn to face the reader and take down the 'No Trespassing' signs. He also publicly admitted his dependence on readers if his poems were "to exist in a practical sense at all". This view of poetry is exceedingly modest and recognises that writing a poem is not an act of the will, an expression of ambition. It puts the poet in the passive or humbling position of waiting to become obsessed before writing a poem and then leaving the fate of the poem to readers.

Larkin wisely avoided defining poetry, much less good poetry. He simply wrote the best poems he could, when he could, based on his experience of poetry and his realisation that poetry had chosen him. And that is the way *The Whitsun Weddings* came to be written – 32 poems produced in about a decade.

I

If 'Church Going' is the centrepiece of *The Less Deceived*, 'MCMXIV' is the centrepiece of *The Whitsun Weddings* – the 16th of the 32 poems in the book. It is a shorter poem than 'Church Going' and the shifts in tone are much less drastic or dramatic. The Larkinesque persona, the 'I' of the poem does not become an 'eye' here, as in 'At Grass', but rather disappears altogether, as if subsumed by the matter of the poem. There is a selflessness about this disappearance, equivalent to the modesty of Larkin's view of poetry: the poet disappears into the work, acknowledging the primacy of the matter of the poem, a reflection of the source of his obsession, and of his potential readers. Larkin also described this poem as a "trick poem", a single long sentence with no main verb. There is nothing gimmicky about this trick, however. A single long sentence with no main verb is the exact grammatical equivalent of the poem's subject – a static moment suspended in time, in history, a time that pre-dates Larkin's birth but with which he identified imaginatively, the poised moment prior to the violent action of World War I, the end of a world, of a way of life.

The title of the poem and its first words – "Those long uneven lines" – suggest the continuity of a culture that culminated in what is described in the single long sentence of the poem. The Roman numerals of the title suggest England's Roman past and also the tendency to express commemorative dates on public buildings or monuments in Roman numerals. "Those long uneven lines" is an accurate description of the lines of volunteers who were to go off to fight in World War I but also family lines, the uneven lineage that had in 1914: produced those recruits: "moustached, archaic faces/ Grinning as if it were all/An August Bank holiday lark". The irony of this statement is marked by an affection for if not an awe of those "archaic faces" much more than by mockery. The poet's identification with them is established by the punning piece of his own name – "lark" – that joins the long, uneven lines of the poem. Still, there is something childlike if not childish about the young men in those lines, "Standing as patiently/As if they were stretched outside/The Oval or Villa Park." The so-called Great War or 'the war to end all wars' does seem to have been viewed at first as a kind of sporting event, a cricket or a football match. There was a sense that it would be over quickly and with little harm done. If anyone foresaw the destruction of a way of life – a destruction that caused Freud to reconsider his ideas on human psychology and admit the existence of a 'death wish' as well as a pleasure principle – they remained relatively silent at the beginning of the war. In this way, Larkin's poem conveys the history of every individual as well as a social history of England – our waiting patiently in lines and going about our business with death, out of mind but inevitable, waiting for us in the end. The single sentence with no main verb of this poem is a death sentence.

As in 'At Grass', there is a cinematic quality to the structure of this poem. It begins with a close-up on the faces in those long, uneven lines, jogs back to take in human artefacts and the children who represent the future, the precarious continuity of the lines, and then stakes in a wide-angle shot to contemplate "the countryside not caring;/The placenames all hazed over/With flowering grasses, and fields/Shadowing Domesday lines/Under wheat's restless silence." The repetition of "lines" at the end of a line here forces the reader to realise that "the countryside", the physical earth of England, literally embodies the past, from Roman times through the names in the Domesday book, to provide the sustenance and the ground on which the present and the future stand. "Domesday", of course, also serves to make clear the seriousness of what at first appeared a mere afternoon at Villa Park like any other. After the fruitful and sustaining image of the wheat, human details appear again, drawing attention to the way life was organised in 1914:

> The differently-dressed servants
> With tiny rooms in huge houses,
> The dust behind limousines.

Once the details are taken in, it is as if the camera stops and the poet speaks, not in images, but in abstractions for which he eventually finds concrete images:

> Never such innocence,
> Never before or since,
> As changed itself to past
> Without a word – the men
> Leaving the gardens tidy,
> The thousands of marriages
> Lasting a little while longer:
> Never such innocence again.

It is unlikely that anyone but Philip Larkin could have written this poem. Scholars have found that some of its properties and images appear in other poems with which Larkin was familiar. That does not matter very much. This is not a poem worked up for publication in order to establish the poet's name. It is the result of a private obsession that has been made fit to appear in public. It is an obsession with a loss of innocence for which no one and nothing is to blame. It is that innocence itself that "changed ... to past/Without a word".

Neither the archaic faces nor the uncaring countryside are responsible for the change. Larkin's aim is neither to analyse nor to blame but to preserve that precariously poised moment of innocence. For this reason, the poem does not end with death and destruction. It does not end at all. It is the result of an obsession with a personal as well as an historic past that has been preserved for anyone who cares to read it in any place and at any time. It is an obsession with men like Larkin's father who left "the gardens tidy" and "The thousands of marriages/Lasting a little while longer." It is an obsession with a time in which Larkin no doubt felt he might have been more at home, a time in which he, too, might have managed to marry and to produce "dark-clothed children at play/Called after kings and queens", children not unlike his sister and himself. It is the human obsession with lost possibilities and potential as much as lost innocence.

Larkin's preference for poets like Thomas Hardy and Edward Thomas shows his attraction to the way of life that ended with World War I. But a 'Freudian slip' he made during an interview shows it even more clearly: "I came on to the labour market in the middle of the First – Christ, I mean the Second World War." He could have easily and silently corrected this slip when he reprinted the interview in a book. He did not do so no doubt because he realised that the slip revealed a good deal about himself as a man and as a poet. Just as he was a non-believer who yearned for religious faith and a bachelor who yearned for marriage and a successful, traditional family life, so was he a thoroughly contemporary representative of the 50s who yearned for the past.

II

If Larkin was an able administrator, like his father, he was also an incompetent, complaining, quasi-hysterical homemaker, like his mother. Friends were shocked by his innocence or ignorance of routine matters of daily life. He could deal with architects, builders, and the political and financial aspects of the administration of a modern university in order to build the kind of library he thought Hull deserved, but if he had to find a place to stay or buy a new carpet he was thrown off his precarious balance and became all but paralysed with indecision and worry. These two aspects of his character run parallel to his opinions and his emotions, his thoughts and his feelings. His poems seem to be the sporadic offspring produced by the brief and uneasy couplings of these two sides of his nature – the male and the female, the classic and the romantic, the comic and the sad. His poems link up and connect, adding up to be more than their individual parts, because they bear a family resemblance. Images recur like the elements of similar but individual faces that are past on from generation to generation in families.

The "lines" of 'MCMXIV' figuratively stretch from the centre of *The Whitsun Weddings* to connect with 'Here', the first poem in the book, and 'An Arundel Tomb', the last poem in it. This is a reversal of the order in which the poems were written – of the three, 'An Arundel Tomb' was written first and 'Here' was written last. What that means is that Larkin, like his early master Yeats, deliberately arranged his poems when he set about making a book of them. In conversation and correspondence he seems to have not made too much of this, suggesting merely that the variety of his forms and subjects should appeal to readers – if they did not like one poem they could turn the page and find something quite different. But just as his individual poems can please 'common readers' on first reading as well as repay the efforts of critics who are willing to devote a good deal of attention to them, so his collections call for consideration as unified wholes rather than random collections of individual poems.

'Here' focuses on a place – a Hull and its environs of the imagination, what has been called 'Larkin country' – in the same way that 'MCMXIV' focuses on a time. But 'Here' implies a time – the now of Larkin's own time, the late 50s and early 60s. The poem imaginatively describes Hull in the realistic present:

> Here domes and statues, spires and cranes cluster
> Beside grain-scattered streets, barge-crowded water,
> And residents from raw estates, brought down
> The dead straight miles by stealing flat-faced trolleys,
> Push through plate-glass swing doors to their desires –
> Cheap suits, red kitchen-ware, sharp shoes, iced lollies,
> Electric mixers, toasters, washers, driers –
>
> A cut-priced crowd, urban yet simple …

The inhabitants of this imaginary Hull are no doubt to be compared with the people in the "uneven lines" of 'MCMXIV' – the unevenness rendered "dead straight" by the tracks of trolleys and the grins of the "archaic faces" lost in the "cut-priced crowd" of "residents." The movement of 'Here', however, is not to Hull but through it. Emerging from it there are other connections with 'MCMXIV' – "Fast-shadowed wheat-fields" and not people standing patiently but:

> ... Here silence stands
> Like heat. Here leaves unnoticed thicken,
> Hidden weeds flower, neglected waters quicken,
> Luminously-peopled air ascends;
> And past the poppies bluish neutral distance
> Ends the land suddenly beyond a beach
> Of shapes and shingle. Here is unfenced existence:
> Facing the sun, untalkative, out of reach.

In this poem there is again no Larkinesque persona, no 'I'. There is only a voice, moving through time and space, piling up a crowd of details, travelling from night to day, and eastward from "traffic all night north" to and through Hull, to where the land ends and the sun is up. There is certainly no envy of the married in this poem. Wives are described as "grim head-scarfed" and are not meant to be attractive partners any more than the "mortgaged half-built edges" of the town are meant to be attractive places to live. The "urban yet simple" confusion of this imaginary Hull is compared with, first, "isolate villages" where "loneliness clarifies" and, finally, "unfenced existence", and suffers from the comparison.

Larkin was once asked if he ever missed being at the centre of things, meaning the centre of literary life in London. He replied, "Oh no, I very much feel the need to be on the periphery of things." This seems to have been perfectly true and natural for him. It is no doubt one of the reasons he never married. He sometimes took young women he worked with cycling or hiking in the countryside around Hull and in some cases began to think about wanting to marry them. But for him to play his natural part and write poems he needed – or thought he needed – the clarity and silence of loneliness and the illusion, at least, of individuality and freedom, of "unfenced existence."

'An Arundel Tomb', on the other hand, is a meditation in the present on a monument to married love in the past, the tomb of an "earl and countess." No 'I' occurs in this poem. Instead, the "plainness of the pre-baroque" tomb "hardly involves the eye" until "One sees, with a sharp tender shock,/His hand withdrawn, holding her hand."

This "sharp tender shock" aroused by physical contact between the effigies of a man and a woman and the sculptor's ability to preserve the contact through his art seem to be the sources of the obsession that caused Larkin to write this poem. For Larkin, that shock is related to falsehood in art and infidelity in marriage. There is a pun in the poem's second line – "The earl and countess lie in stone", a reference to the physical position of the statues and to the falsehood they seem to state, the fundamental falsehood of remaining visible in stone after they have been dead and gone for generations but also the potential falsehood of appearing to be faithful lovers when they had, in life, been guilty of infidelity.

On the personal level, this subject no doubt confronts again the tangle of emotions that kept Larkin from marrying or enjoying a full sexual life. It seems likely that he was aware of rumours that his father had indulged in what would now be called sexual harassment at his office, if not actual affairs. Larkin himself seems to have had one of his most satisfactory, if brief, relationships with the wife of a friend and colleague in Belfast. On the public level, the subject confronts the way the public pose of a married couple can be the false image of a very different private life. In the most general terms, the poem deals with how a work of art – a tomb or a poem – changes through time, as "succeeding eyes begin/To look, not read", either because they can no longer read the Latin on the tomb or simply because the way of life fixed in the work of art is gone, so that its viewers are no longer "friends" but "endless altered people", the inhabitants of a changed future, reminiscent of both the "uneven lines" of men in 'MCMXIV' and the "cut-price crowd" of 'Here'. Despite all these doubts and hedges, Larkin concludes the poem with a sceptical and hedged generalisation:

> Time has transfigured them into
> Untruth. The stone fidelity
> They hardly meant has come to be
> Their final blazon, and to prove

Our almost-instinct almost true:
What will survive of us is love.

The fate of this poem has been similar to the fate Larkin found in the tomb itself. The final line, free of doubts, hedges, or qualifications, is what people carry away from the poem and remember. What he "hardly meant" and never could live by or live up to for long has become one of the final blazons for which he is remembered. Its placement at the end of the poem and at the end of the volume sealed the line's fate.

III

'Here', 'MCMXIV', and 'An Arundel Tomb' give *The Whitsun Weddings* a relatively objective beginning, middle, and end. They are all spoken in the present but with a growing awareness of history, the past, and the twists and turns, the changes, they contain. In a way, the volume moves from present loneliness, through marriages in the past that lasted because of innocence, to a contemplation of married love still further back, based on the acceptance of 'art' and falsehood. The spaces between these landmarks, as it were, are filled with a surprising variety of poems.

The Larkinesque persona first established in *The Less Deceived* remains very much in evidence in 'Mr Bleaney', 'Toads Revisited', a direct link with the previous collection, the title poem, 'The Whitsun Weddings', 'Dockery and Son', and 'Wild Oats'. 'Love Songs in Age' and 'Reference Back' deal with Larkin's loyal but strained relationship with his mother. 'Broadcast' and 'Talking in Bed' are love poems that seem to be addressed to Maeve Brennan and Monica Jones respectively. Larkin's private or emotional life seems to have centred on his mother and Monica Jones as constants to be kept at a distance and on various younger women who at times appeared as potential wives. The difficulty of knowing or telling the truth, a theme of 'An Arundel Tomb', finds tender expression in 'Talking in Bed' and sardonic expression in 'Send No Money', a poem which ends with characteristically alliterative and bitter lines.

Larkin in early middle age became increasingly aware of illness, age, and death because of his need to help care for his mother and because of his own relatively frequent sickness and occasional hospitalisations. This awareness produced such poems as 'Nothing To Be Said', 'Faith Healing', 'Ambulances', and 'Sunny Prestatyn'. But *The Whitsun Weddings* also contains two brief lyric poems that seem to have arisen miraculously, with few detailed references to the actual day-to-day reality of England in the 50s and 60s or to Larkin's actual life. They somehow contain or convey the innocence that 'MCMXIV' announced was gone for good. They are two of the earliest poems in the book – 'Water', written when Larkin was still in Belfast, and 'First Sight', written about a year after he arrived in Hull. These modest, simple poems, despite their similarities, have some differences. 'Water' is written in the first-person singular but with little of the pose or characterisation of the Larkinesque persona. It is sheer utterance, blending humour and seriousness, and spoken with a sense of urgency and inevitability so that the flow of the words give the poem its shape.

'First Sight' has the appearance of a made poem when it is compared with 'Water'. It consists of two seven-line stanzas of rhymed trochaic tetrameter. All of its rhymes are full and most of them, with the exception of that important word for Larkin, "surprise", are monosyllabic. The first and last lines end with the same word, "snow", suggesting a circle of continuity that contains even surprising changes. The time of year depicted is the same as that in 'Coming', the first stirrings of spring that occur at the end of winter. The newborn lambs of the poem are realistically presented and yet serve as symbols of innocence and ignorance. Larkin loses himself in these lambs in much the same way that he lost himself in the horses of 'At Grass'.

'First Sight' is one of the poems that, like John Kemp's fantasy life, set Kingsley Amis to pondering. He found it impossible to reconcile this poem with the "visible Philip". Poems like this one, if not typical of Larkin, are an integral part of his work and set him apart from his contemporaries. Not one of them is likely to have wanted to write this kind of poem. The simplicity, potential sentimentality, and old-fashionedness of it probably would have embarrassed them. They did not embarrass Larkin. These "newly stumbling" lines have an anonymous quality – a quality they share with Elizabethan songs, nursery rhymes, and old ballads. They also have a timeless quality – they could have been written well before 1914 but continue to remain fresh long after they were actually written. They are the poetic evidence that, in Maeve Brennan's words, "his sympathy was genuine".

III

Larkin once told his mother that he thought he had something in common with his grandfather who seems to have enjoyed "solitary ecstasies". Some of Larkin's "solitary ecstasies" came from his passion for American jazz, a passion celebrated in *The Whitsun Weddings* in a poem entitled 'For Sidney Bechet', the clarinettist and soprano saxophonist from New Orleans. In that poem, Larkin makes clear that jazz, like the "toad *work*", helped him to endure his difficulties with love: "On me your voice falls as they say love should,/Like an enormous yes." This passion led him to begin a third career as a reviewer of jazz records at the time when he was writing some of the poems gathered in *The Whitsun Weddings*.

Although some of these reviews were eventually published in a book, *All What Jazz*, they would have no place in a brief survey of Larkin's life and work if he had not written an 'Introduction' to them. That 'Introduction', part memoir, part polemic, came to be seen as an anti-modernist manifesto, the witty work of a master of English prose. It also has much in common with the style of Larkin's poetry and the public role he increasingly came to play. Soon after he agreed to review the records he found that he could not stand what by the early 60s had come to be called jazz. He described the dilemma this way:

> When the records, in their exciting square packages, began obligingly to arrive from the companies, the eagerness with which I played them turned rapidly to astonishment, to disbelief, to alarm. I felt I was in some nightmare, in which I had confidently gone into an examination hall only to find that I couldn't make head or tail of the questions. It wasn't like listening to a kind of jazz I didn't care for – Art Tatum, shall I say, or Jelly Roll Morton's Red Hot Peppers. It wasn't like listening to jazz at all. Nearly every characteristic of the music had been neatly inverted: for instance, the jazz tone, distinguished from 'straight' practice by an almost-human vibrato, had entirely disappeared, giving way to utter

flaccidity. Had the most original feature of jazz been its use of collective improvisation? Banish it: let the first and last choruses be identical exercises in low-temperature unison. Was jazz instrumentation based on the hock-shop trumpets, trombones and clarinets of the returned Civil War regiments? Brace yourself for flutes, harpsichords, electronically-amplified bassoons. Had jazz been essentially a popular art, full of tunes you could whistle? Something fundamentally awful had taken place to ensure that there should be no more tunes. Had the wonderful thing about it been its happy, cake-walky syncopation that set feet tapping and shoulders jerking? Any such feelings were now regularly dispelled by random explosions from the drummer ('dropping bombs') and the use of non-jazz tempos, 3/4, 5/8, 11/4. Above all, was jazz the music of the American Negro? Then fill it full of conga drums and sambas and all the tawdry trappings of South America, the racket of Middle East bazaars, the cobra-coaxing cacophonies of Calcutta.

Clive James drew attention to the witty use of alliteration to end this paragraph with a flourish and compared it to the well-known closing lines of 'Send No Money':

What does it prove? Sod all.
In this way I spent youth,
Tracing the trite untransferable
Truss-advertisement, truth.

In an attempt to resolve his dilemma, Larkin began to read about jazz. Those books helped to clarify the situation not so much by what they said as by the words they used to say it:

... there was something about the books I was now reading that seemed oddly familiar. This development, this progress, this new language that was more difficult, more complex, that required you to work hard at appreciating it, that you couldn't expect to understand first go, that needed technical and professional knowledge to evaluate it at all levels, this revolutionary explosion that spoke for our time while at the same time being traditional in the fullest, the deepest ... Of course! This was the language of modern painting, modern poetry, modern music. Of course! How glibly I had talked of modern jazz, without realising the force of the adjective: this was modern jazz, and Parker was a modern jazz player just as Picasso was a modern painter and Pound a modern poet. I hadn't realised that jazz had gone from Lascaux to Jackson Pollock in 50 years, but now I realised it relief came flooding in upon me after nearly two years' despondency. I went back to my books: After Parker, you had to be something of a musician to follow the best jazz of the day. Of course! After Picasso! After Pound! There could hardly have been a conciser summary of what I don't believe about art.

With this enlightenment he was prepared to move rapidly to a generalisation:

All I am saying is that the term 'modern', when applied to art, has a more than chronological meaning: it denotes a quality of irresponsibility peculiar to this century, known sometimes as modernism, and once I had classified modern jazz under this heading I knew where I was. I am sure there are books in which the genesis of modernism is set out in full. My own theory is that it is related to an imbalance between the two tensions from which art springs: these are the tension between the artist and his material, and between the artist and his audience, and that in the last 75 years or so the second of these has slackened or even perished. In consequence the artist has become over-concerned with his material (hence an age of experiment), and, in isolation, has busied himself with the two principal themes of modernism, mystification and outrage.

At the end of the 'Introduction', Larkin expressed his gratitude for having been born when he was because of the pleasure he derived from jazz: " ... when I imagine how much I would have missed if, instead of being born on 9th August 1922 I had died then, I realise how great my debt is. How dreadful to have lived in the twentieth century, but died before King Oliver led his men into the Gennett studios at Richmond, Indiana, or before Frank Walker auditioned Bessie Smith ('fat and scared to death') or Bubber Miley joined Duke Ellington's Washingtonians!" This statement necessarily caused him to think of his readers. He concluded by imagining them. It is hard to believe that he did not think of them as the readers of his poems as well as of his record reviews:

... Sometimes I imagine them, sullen fleshy inarticulate men, stockbrokers, sellers of goods, living in thirty-year-old detached houses among the golf courses of Outer London, husbands of ageing and bitter wives they first seduced to Artie Shaw's 'Begin the Beguine' or The Squadronaires 'The Nearness of You'; fathers of cold-eyed lascivious daughters on the pill, to whom Ramsay Macdonald is coeval with Ramses II, and cannabis-smoking jeans-and-bearded Stuart-haired sons whose oriental contempt for 'bread' is equalled only by their insatiable demand for it; men in whom a pile of scratched coverless 78s in the attic can awaken memories of vomiting blindly from small Tudor windows to Muggsy Spanier's 'Sister Kate', or winding up a gramophone in a punt to play Armstrong's 'Body and Soul'; men whose first coronary is coming like Christmas; who drift, loaded helplessly with commitments and obligations and necessary observances, into the darkening avenues of age and incapacity, deserted by everything that once made life sweet. These I have tried to remind of the excitement of jazz, and tell where it may still be found.

He wrote for readers who were very much like himself and his friends at school or at Oxford during the war or, rather, who were very much like what they had become. If he became a 'reactionary' it was to wage a rear-guard action to preserve the memory of what "once made life sweet" for him and them. And he did it with humour. He advised his publishers to treat *All What Jazz* the way they would "a book by T.S. Eliot on all-in wrestling."

4   *High Windows*

Larkin felt a certain amount of embarrassment about the fame and popularity he gained following the publication of *The Whitsun Weddings*. There was no false modesty about this. He was well aware of the quality of his work and the nature of his achievement. He simply saw that work and that achievement against the backdrop of the work of the poets he admired most – not only Thomas Hardy, William Barnes, Edward Thomas, Wilfred Owen, and Christina Rossetti, but also the Americans – Walt Whitman and Robert Frost.

Early in his career, when reviewers praised the work of Larkin and his contemporaries in *New Lines,* the anthology edited by Robert Conquest, Larkin's head was not turned. He wrote to Conquest with admirable honesty to point out that the poems in the anthology did not measure up to the high standard set by the best poems of the past. Later, he would argue that he wrote too little and not well enough, only "twenty times better than anybody else." This combination of modesty and arrogance results in a surprising accuracy. He was, as many critics repeatedly said in print, one of the best poets in English of his time. But his time was not a particularly good one for poetry.

Worry about the quality and amount of what he wrote was no affectation. The last collection of his poems to appear in his lifetime – *High Windows* (1974) – was also his briefest and bleakest volume. The book's brevity and bleakness are clearly related to the themes that dominate the collection – a growing concern with illness, age, and death, an increasing lack of sympathy with his time, and a loss of inspiration. Larkin had outgrown his stammer, but his hearing became progressively worse so that he had to be fitted with two hearing aids. He maintained constant contact with his widowed mother and watched closely the effects of old age on her. He also confided to some friends the fear he felt of a loss of inspiration, a loss of the ability to write poems. And the once new spirit in literature he represented was beginning to go out of fashion, to be replaced by a yet newer style or, perhaps more accurately, an eclectic mix of styles. Larkin's life and the themes it forced him to face did not lead to unrelieved bleakness, however. He faced his themes with clarity but also humour and lyricism. If the humour became more angry and bitter, the lyricism remained as sweet and unselfconscious as ever.

'The Old Fools' combines angry, bitter humour and lyricism to face old age and death squarely. The neatly rhymed stanzas are as skilful as those Larkin produced earlier in his career – in 'Church Going' or 'The Whitsun Weddings' – but there are fewer of them. The poem consists of four twelve-line stanzas. This relative brevity of the poem reflects its treatment of its subject. The best of Larkin's poems begin with necessity, obsession, and end with discovery, knowledge. In 'The Old Fools', in part because of the theme but also because of failing inspiration, the poem ends where it begins, with unanswered and perhaps unanswerable questions – what it is like to be old and on the verge of death, "crowding below/ Extinction's alp", in a hospital or nursing home. The only answer to this question comes in the final line of the poem, "We shall find out" – no answer at all, because speculation on the subject is useless. It requires experience. Despite this conclusion, the speculations that make up the poem do have a use, serve a purpose. They allow the poet and the reader to move from sardonic mockery of the old to a sympathetic understanding of them and the realisation that 'we' – no matter what our age, health, or mental condition – are one with them, doomed to the same end, facing the same experience.

The poem opens with an angry impatience with the old, but expressed with the kind of frankness that combines anger with laughter:

> What do they think has happened, the old fools,
> To make them like this? Do they somehow suppose
> It's more grown-up when your mouth hangs open and drools,
> And you keep on pissing yourself, and can't remember
> Who called this morning?

Larkin had made himself notorious on the subject of children, publicly complaining that they are "cruel, noisy, selfish brutes" and so on. His anger and disgust with the aged seems to have sprung from the same impulse. The virtues he admired – clarity, precision, modesty, reasonableness, and independence – seemed to him to exist neither in the young nor the old. He was primarily a poet of the middle-aged and the middle-class – the men he imagined as his readers in the 'Introduction' to *All What Jazz*. He was an opponent of extremes – outlandishness in thought and behaviour. The old, like the young, were incapable of reasonableness and given to outlandishness. Larkin explodes the cliché of old age as a 'second childhood' by taking it seriously.

In an early poem, published in *The Less Deceived,* Larkin made clear his awareness that, "Beneath it all, desire for oblivion runs". This awareness does not imply a simple 'death wish'. On the contrary, Larkin strongly felt the attractions of the 'all'. It is that sense that produces the rational lyricism in the second stanza of 'The Old Fools':

> At death, you break up: the bits that were you
> Start speeding away from each other for ever
> With no one to see. It's only oblivion, true:
> We had it before, but then it was going to end,
> And was all the time merging with a unique endeavour
> To bring to bloom the million-petalled flower
> Of being here.

It is the uniqueness of each individual and the fragile beauty of "the million-petalled flower/Of being here" that Larkin finds insulted by life's end. It is the silent, befuddled acceptance of this insult by the old that frames his primary questions, "Why aren't they screaming?" and "How can they ignore it?" His attitude softens when he considers that the old are drawn to live in the past, with the dead:

> Perhaps being old is having lighted rooms
> Inside your head, and people in them, acting.
> People you know, yet can't quite name; each looms
> Like a deep loss restored, from known doors turning,
> Setting down a lamp, smiling from a stair, extracting
> A known book from the shelves.

This dwelling on the remembered ordinary details of life that make up the "million-petalled flower" of each individual existence helps to explain the "air of baffled absence" of the old, their attempt to live in the past while moving towards death. The poet's identification with the old fools never becomes complete, however. Despite his tentative answers to the questions they raise for him, he is driven to renewed questioning:

> … Can they never tell
> What is dragging them back, and how it will end? Not at night?
> Not when the strangers come? Never, throughout
> The whole hideous inverted childhood?

It is this series of questions that remains unanswerable and leads to the grim resignation, tinged with horror, "We shall find out." The inability to make a discovery – equivalent to the "surprising" discovery of a "hunger to be more serious" in 'Church-Going' or the "almostinstinct" of "What will survive of us is love" in 'An Arundel Tomb' – makes several of the most ambitious poems in *High Windows,* 'The Old Fools', 'The Building', 'To the Sea', and 'Show Saturday' weaker than their counterparts in earlier volumes. The best known of Larkin's poems in this collection became popular for non-poetic reasons. 'This Be The Verse' with its startling opening lines and its conclusion of versified Schopenhauer and "Annus Mirabilis" with its comic and curmudgeonly first stanza:

> Sexual intercourse began
> In nineteen sixty-three
> (Which was rather late for me) –
> Between the end of the Chatterley ban
> And the Beatles' first LP

come dangerously close to light verse, expressions of the Larkinesque persona playing to what had become one segment of his audience.

It is not that Larkin had lost his way or lost his ear. It is rather that his inspiration was flagging and he was aware of that. He is to be admired for not merely turning out tired verses or self-parodies. As he wrote in a letter to one of his oldest friends, he could no doubt "fudge" something up but he found doing so no replacement for the "true urge." He deals with the loss of inspiration and its social implications in one of the best and funniest poems in *High Windows,* 'Vers de Société'. In a way, 'Vers de Société' revisits 'Church-Going' through the suggestion that social life has become a modern equivalent of going to church. In this poem, as in the early one, the Larkinesque persona begins with mockery, undergoes a change of heart, but ends with ironic resignation rather than with communal exaltation. The comedy of the poem at first takes the form of a satiric parody of a dinner invitation:

> *My wife and I have asked a crowd of craps*
> *To come and waste their time and ours; perhaps*
> *You'd care to join us?* In a pig's arse, friend.
> Day comes to an end.
> The gas fire breathes, the trees are darkly swayed.
> And so *Dear Warlock-Williams: I'm afraid –*

Larkin, because of his job, wrote his poems in the evening, after work. He lived for 18 years in the same flat at the top of a house with windows facing a park. He wrote most of the poems in *The Whitsun Weddings* and *High Windows* while living there. He used 'High Windows' as the title of a poem and a collection because it defines his point of view, literally, when he wrote – isolated, an observer with a vantage point from which it is hard to be observed, above society, contemplating the park, the trees and the sky through glass. Poetry is a kind of outspokenness and Larkin clearly believed it to be asocial if not anarchic, despite its reliance on readers, requiring solitude as well as dedication. The well-meant invitation is fiercely parodied because it is prose, the language of society, and cannot compare to the attractions of poetry, words that are uncalled-for, that come of their own volition, as it were – a matching of the inner and the outer worlds through the movement of breath. Inspiration is conveyed by the images in the single line: "The gas fire breathes, the trees are darkly swayed". This opening necessarily leads to a consideration of society and poetry as opposites, with the demands of the former diminishing the opportunities for the latter. Larkin makes this point by rapidly following the comic with the lyric, a satiric glance at chat about "modern literature" followed by the actuality of poetry:

> I could spend half my evenings, if I wanted,
> Holding a glass of washing sherry, canted
> Over to catch the drivel of some bitch
> Who's read nothing but *Which*;
> Just think of all the spare time that has flown

Straight into nothingness by being filled
With forks and faces, rather than repaid
Under a lamp, hearing the noise of wind,
And looking out to see the moon thinned
To an air-sharpened blade.

The difference between "the drivel of some bitch" and "the noise of wind" is the difference between society and poetry. Two italicised phrases, the voice of society, an instructive, parental voice, come down on the side of society: "*All solitude is selfish*" and "*Virtue is social*". These moral or ethical statements are what cause Larkin to compare taking part in social life with going to church:

Are, then, these routines

Playing at goodness, like going to church?
Something that bores us, something we don't do well
(Asking that ass about his fool research)
But try to feel, because, however crudely,
It shows us what should be?

He rejects this identification on the ground it is "too subtle" and "too decent". But this rejection leads him to face his own situation – his increasing age and his failing inspiration:

Only the young can be alone freely.
The time is shorter now for company,
And sitting by a lamp more often brings
Not peace, but other things.
Beyond the light stand failure and remorse
Whispering *Dear Warlock-Williams: Why, of course –*

The poem ends with an ironic acceptance of the social because Larkin had the honesty never to lose sight of the fact that poetry had chosen him and so could choose to leave him. It is this fact that causes sitting under a lamp at this stage of his life to bring him "not peace" but the whispering of failure and remorse. 'Vers de Société' is not light, social verse at all. It is a moving confession of failing inspiration, honestly presented, and made bearable by Larkin's comic gift and lingering lyric ability. He was not prepared to equate poetry with modern literature or learning ("Asking that ass about his fool research") or goodness as defined by society or the popular success that increases the social whirl. He knew that poetry was less like these things than like the noise of the wind or the sight of the moon as perceived by a solitary individual. But like the wind and the moon it was not at his beck and call.

Despite the irony, he clearly felt the companionship of "failure and remorse." The irony was no doubt heightened for him by the public acclamation and honours that continued to come his way when he hardly thought of himself as a poet any longer at all. Soon after the publication of *High Windows* he openly reported in interviews that he rarely wrote poems and did not expect to produce much more. He sometimes attributed this failure of inspiration to the need to give up the flat he had lived in for years with its high windows and move into a house. Owning a home, like marriage, seemed to represent for him one of those decisions that link a person firmly to society and thus jeopardise poetry. But he had earlier confided to friends the fear that poetry would leave him at the age of 50, that is, in 1972, shortly before the publication of *High Windows*. These kinds of statements can sound like mere superstition, a way of making excuses. They are not. They are the best guesses of a poet who understood and tried to accept his own limitations and strengths.

There are still surprising strengths in *High Windows*. Larkin always had the ability to coin lines that immediately lodged in the memories of readers. He also always had the ability to be critical of the way of life around him, applying the standard he had announced in 'Mr Bleaney' – "how we live measures our own nature." And he also continued to produce true if modest poems. 'Dublinesque' is one of those. Larkin told Maeve Brennan that 'Dublinesque' was the accurate transcription of a dream and that he was able to write it out quickly. The poem concludes:

> As they wend away
> A voice is heard singing
> Of Kitty, or Katy,
> As if the name meant once
> All love, all beauty.

The distant voice singing a talismanic name is the voice of poetry. Larkin's biographer, not Jake Balokowsky but Andrew Motion, drew attention to the fact that the names Kitty or Katy were names of Larkin's sister, Catherine. What he does not point out is that the names in 'Dublinesque' are applied to a prostitute, a woman mourned by "a troop of streetwalkers." The appearance of the names in this context suggest that Larkin's dream was part of the fantasy life of "invisible Philip", emerging from the private life that had earlier produced John Kemp's fantasies and the story of Katherine Lind and shaped Larkin's bachelorhood and his attitudes toward women. Those attitudes were among the sources of controversy that came to surround Larkin's posthumous reputation.

5 Achievement and Reputation

In pre-literate cultures, poets are the repositories of the culture's memory and as such are charged with the responsibility of rendering public judgements – blessing and blasting, praising and satirising. Poets help bind the culture together and define and preserve its sense of order, its sense of appropriate behaviour. That public, social role for poetry has long since disappeared in modern society, not only literate but clogged with constant effusions from the mass media. Poets now provide a relatively small segment of the population with a specialised kind of reading matter, a potential pleasure that some people continue to prefer to other ways of spending leisure time. As Larkin was very much aware, this relatively small segment of the population has been artificially inflated by what he called "subsidising poetry", state financial support for the arts, education, and cultural activities. One result of this inflation has been for some poets who are basically private, even marginal figures to be put in the false position of continuing to play a public role. To say that poets are private, even marginal figures is not to say that they are unimportant. On the contrary, it is at least arguable that, in our time, their importance increases the more private and marginal they are. If bards were important because they spoke from the centre of the charmed circle of a tribal culture, poets are important today because they view themselves and their society from a strictly personal, even idiosyncratic slant. In an age of mass media, poetry preserves the voice of an individual addressing individuals, rather than an anonymous mass addressing an anonymous mass.

This shifting role of poets and poetry has produced confusion about how we are to understand and judge the work and lives of poets. There is a desire for poets to be 'sound', that is, for their opinions and habits to be admirable from the point of view of society. There is also the desire for poets to be colourful figures, eccentric and bohemian, who gleefully thumb their noses at conventions and conventional opinions. In both cases, the conventions of society rather than of poetry are used as the basis for judgement. Larkin's posthumous reputation has suffered more than most from this confusion. Once credited with being a popular poet who had reconnected poetry with a relatively large audience, it has now been seriously suggested that his work should not be read in schools because he was a sexist, a racist, and a closet Nazi with peculiar sexual kinks. Both views are serious exaggerations that have little to do with Larkin's poems.

I said at the outset that Larkin was praised by judicious critics following the publication of *The Less Deceived*. That is certainly true, but the critical appraisal of Larkin's work was never unanimous. From the very beginning there were dissenting voices, muttering about the 'middlebrow muse' and complaining about the 'low temperature' or 'low intensity' of Larkin's work. These critics simply resented what others found attractive – the language and properties drawn from 'ordinary' life, the absence of exotic knowledge, the humour, the versatile but unselfconscious use of traditional poetic forms. These critics seem to have liked the idea of poetry as a 'highbrow' speciality, a kind of museum of verbal objets d'art. This antagonism to Larkin's poems and public stance grew with his reputation. For some, his 'Introduction' to *All What Jazz* was the turning point. Critics and fellow poets who more or less thought of themselves as aesthetes were shocked and repelled by what they took to be Larkin's philistinism. His attacks on Picasso and Ezra Pound, reminiscent of the point of view of the mythical 'man in the street', struck them as a kind of treachery – a man of culture denouncing the culture of his time by abusing two of its international heroes. This view seemed to find support in Larkin's overt insularity – his distaste for 'abroad' and his pride in his apparent ignorance of poetry in foreign languages. And this at a time when other English poets were flitting around the world on intercontinental flights and bulking up their books with translations. Larkin began to look eccentric.

His edition of *The Oxford Book of Twentieth Century English Verse* (1973) was the thick straw that broke the camel's back for still other critics and poets. Robert Lowell, the American poet charmingly defended the book as "a work of art" by Philip Larkin and therefore idiosyncratic but interesting. Donald Davie, who had been associated with Larkin as a member of 'The Movement', reported "recoiling aghast" from page after page of the book and indulged in lengthy diatribes against it. The uproar surrounding the anthology seems to have been based again on Larkin's philistinism, his opposition to modernism and his attraction for the forgotten, the peripheral, the insular – a preference for rhyming poems about animals by unknown or unfashionable poets, for instance. The book made the divergent views of Larkin and his critics clear. His aim was to make a readable bedside book from the mass of English poems produced in this century. His critics thought his aim should have been to establish a volume of approved or acceptable English poems for the century.

All of these controversies and disillusionments were as nothing compared with what came following the publication of the *Selected Letters of Philip Larkin: 1940-1985,* edited by Anthony Thwaite, in 1992, and *Philip Larkin: A Writer's Life* by Andrew Motion, in 1993. The outrage and horror at the revelations contained in these two books was one additional indication of how much affection people had felt for Larkin. There was a sense of personal shock and betrayal when people learned that the author of poems they admired was a devotee of pornography, an outspoken opponent of immigration, a loather of the working class and the welfare state, a vehement anti-Communist, and a despiser of the young, especially of the radical young of the 60s and 70s who had been taught to read and revere him. He was also seen to have been an ambitious poet capable of vicious attacks on his contemporaries. It was as if the masters at King Henry VIII School, Coventry, convinced of Larkin's politeness, even his courtliness, suddenly overheard him doing wickedly, mercilessly funny imitations of them for his friends. The hurt, disappointment, anger, and confusion arose from a confusion of the public and the private lives. Larkin's inhibited, unhappy life should have come as a surprise to no one. What offended was the appearance in public of private opinions, quirks, and vices that ran contrary to prevailing views in intellectual circles – what might best be called the liberationist ethic of universal love and understanding, an ethic with little tolerance for individuals, only abstractions.

The question to be asked of a contemporary poet's private life is not whether it is admirable or exemplary or consistent with fashionable trends, but whether it fits that poet's work – is one with that work. There is no question that Philip Larkin's life and work are of a piece. "I think that one of the great criticisms of poets of the past", he told an interviewer, "is that they said one thing and did another, a false relation between art and life. I always try to avoid this." He did avoid it to an extraordinary degree. And he avoided it through what Kingsley Amis called his "frightening honesty." It is that honesty that gives his poems the breath of life, an individual cadence and a distinctive point of view, and gives the records of his private life a brutal frankness, at once comic and sad, cruel and sentimental, charming and repugnant. There is no need to defend his opinions or proclivities. They were what they were. But it would be a disservice not to take them seriously, to pretend they were simply expressed as jokes, or to argue that they were separate and distinct from his poems.

As Penelope Fitzgerald, the biographer and novelist, wrote in a review of *The Selected Letters*:

> More distressing by far [than his looking at "girlie magazines", his drinking, and his cracks about literary figures] are his general opinions, forcibly expressed, which leave the whole concept of political incorrectness gasping. If they represent what he really or even sometimes felt, immigration (Letting The Buggers In Here) must be made illegal before every household in the land is overrun, unemployment should be got rid of by stopping national assistance, workingmen are "awful shits marching or picketing" the Labour Party are Communists who would like to see him in a camp for dissidents ... How seriously were his correspondents supposed to take all this? I think quite seriously. When I was working in an unimportant capacity for the British Arts Council Literary Panel, Larkin was asked for advice on the funding of ethnic arts centres. He replied that anyone lucky enough to be allowed to settle here had a duty to forget their own culture and try to understand ours.

Kingsley Amis' distinction between "visible Philip" and "invisible Philip" is likely to take us as far as we can currently go in understanding Larkin based on the voluminous but limited evidence that is so far available. (Larkin's letters to his father, mother, and sister like those to Bruce Montgomery, 'Edmund Crispin', and many of those to Monica Jones and Kingsley Amis, have not yet been published. His massive diaries were apparently destroyed at his own request immediately after his death on 2nd December 1985.)

The opinions, tone of voice, and habits that shocked people were primarily those of "visible Philip", the "non-gamesplaying hearty" as Amis said or "one of nature's Orangemen", as Larkin himself put it. The pugnacity of this no-nonsense figure is neither witless nor purposeless. It is extremely witty and its purpose is the same as that Larkin assigned to the writing of poems – to preserve. What that pugnacity publicly wished to preserve was an England that was past, a way of life that had been destroyed. He described it in 'Going, Going', a poem in *High Windows:*

> For the first time I feel somehow
> That it isn't going to last,
>
> That before I snuff it, the whole
> Boiling will be bricked in
> Except for the tourist parts –
> First slum of Europe: a role
> It won't be so hard to win,
> With a cast of crooks and tarts.
>
> And that will be England gone,
> The shadows, the meadows, the lanes,
> The guildhalls, the carved choirs.
> There'll be books; it will linger on
> In galleries; but all that remains
> For us will be concrete and tyres.

He seems to have used that same pugnacity privately to preserve "invisible Philip", not the joking, drinking, outspoken companion of Kingsley Amis and Robert Conquest, but the lonely, unhappy, insecure bachelor, the loyal but frustrated son, perhaps even more sexually ambivalent than the record so far shows, who at times felt the "true urge" and wrote lyrics like 'Cut Grass' from *High Windows,* lyrics that seem to suggest he somehow contrived to live in an imagined England that remained untouched by time and history.

'Bitterly outspoken Philip' and 'unselfconsciously lyrical Philip' were two aspects of the same person. To reject the one is to diminish if not to reject the other. To reject either because of opinions expressed in private letters to old friends or because of repugnance with the defensive postures of a frightened, lonely man would be to prefer social conventions to poetry. When Larkin was prematurely ageing and losing the ability to write poems, he used his public influence not to outlaw immigration or abolish the dole but to encourage, defend, and urge the publication of the novels of Barbara Pym, to preserve the manuscripts of contemporary writers, and to improve the university libraries of Britain. When he could no longer produce literature, he remained useful to literature. The dignified, useful, but painful silence of his last years is the real evidence of his integrity as a poet. And that stance is of a piece with the last long poem he published, 'Aubade', a clear-eyed anatomization of his horror of death that he finished soon after his mother's death in November 1977.

Larkin's life as a poet seems to be intimately tied to, and circumscribed by, the deaths of his parents. He was born as a poet with his father's death and all but died as a poet when his mother died. In between, for almost thirty years, he wrote roughly three good poems a year, on average – poems that only he could have written. Of how many of his contemporaries can as much be said? This is not to claim that Larkin was a 'great' poet or a 'major' poet – terms that become increasingly meaningless and misleading. It is to say that he produced a number of poems that are likely to attract readers for as long as English is read. It would not surprise me if many of these prove to be modest lyrics, the outpourings of "invisible Philip", rather than those poems that most helped to fuel the blaze of his contemporary fame. Fame, like neglect, no doubt has its price. Larkin's exaggerated reputation in his lifetime probably meant that a reaction against it was inevitable. It is a pity that that reaction is now likely to be similarly exaggerated. But Larkin knew that the fate of his poems ultimately rests with readers – not commentators, critics, or scholars. He should have the last word here:

> I should hate anybody to read my work because he's been told to and told what to think about it. I really want to hit them, I want readers to feel yes, I've never thought of it that way, but that's how it is.

Selected Bibliography

Books by Philip Larkin
A Girl in Winter (Faber and Faber, 1947)
All What Jazz (Faber and Faber, 1970)
Collected Poems, ed. Anthony Thwaite (Faber and Faber and The
　　Marvell Press, 1988)
Jill (Faber and Faber, 1976; rpt of 1946 Fortune Press edition)
Required Writing: Miscellaneous Pieces 1955-1982 (Faber and
　　Faber, 1983)
Selected Letters of Philip Larkin: 1940-1985, ed. Anthony Thwaite
　　(Faber and Faber, 1992)

Books about Philip Larkin
Anthony Thwaite, ed. *Larkin At Sixty* (Faber and Faber, 1982)
Dale Salwak, ed. *Philip Larkin: The Man and His Work* (University
　　of Iowa Press, 1989)
Andrew Motion, *Philip Larkin: A Writer's Life* (Faber and Faber,
　　1993)

GREENWICH EXCHANGE BOOKS

STUDENT GUIDES

Greenwich Exchange Student Guides are critical studies of major or contemporary serious writers in English and selected European languages. The series is for the student, the teacher and 'common readers' and is an ideal resource for libraries. The *Times Educational Supplement* (*TES*) praised these books saying, "The style of these guides has a pressure of meaning behind it. Students should learn from that ... If art is about selection, perception and taste, then this is it."

(ISBN prefix 1-871551- applies)
The series includes:
W. H. Auden by Stephen Wade (-36-6)
Balzac by Wendy Mercer (48-X)
William Blake by Peter Davies (-27-7)
The Brontës by Peter Davies (-24-2)
Joseph Conrad by Martin Seymour-Smith (-18-8)
William Cowper by Michael Thorn (-25-0)
Charles Dickens by Robert Giddings (-26-9)
John Donne by Sean Haldane (-23-4)
Thomas Hardy by Sean Haldane (-33-1)
Seamus Heaney by Warren Hope (-37-4)
Philip Larkin by Warren Hope (-35-8)
Laughter in the Dark - The Plays of Joe Orton by Arthur Burke (56-0)
Shakespeare's Non-Dramatic Poetry by Martin Seymour-Smith (22-6)
Shakespeare's Sonnets by Martin Seymour Smith (38-2)
Tobias Smollett by Robert Giddings (-21-8)
Alfred Lord Tennyson by Michael Thorn (-20-X)
Wordsworth by Andrew Keanie (57-9)

OTHER GREENWICH EXCHANGE BOOKS
Paperback unless otherwise stated.

English Language Skills *by Vera Hughes*
If you want to be sure, as a student, or in your business or personal life, that your written English is correct and up-to-date, this book is for you. Vera Hughes's aim is to help you remember the basic rules of spelling, grammar and punctuation. 'Noun', 'verb', 'subject', 'object' and 'adjective' are the only technical terms used. The book teaches the clear, accurate English required by the business and office world, coaching in acceptable

current usage, and making the rules easier to remember.

With a degree in modern languages and trained as a legal secretary, Vera Hughes went from the City into training with the retail industry before joining MSC as a Senior Training Advisor. As an experienced freelance trainer, she has worked at all levels throughout the UK and overseas, training business people in communication skills, but specialising in written business English. As former Regional Manager for RSA Examinations Board, she is also aware of the needs of students in schools and colleges. Her sound knowledge of English and her wide business experience are an ideal combination for a book about basic English language skills.
ISBN 1-871551-60-9; A5 size; 142pp

LITERATURE & BIOGRAPHY
The Author, the Book & the Reader *by Robert Giddings*
This collection of essays analyses the effects of changing technology and the attendant commercial pressures on literary styles and subject matter. Authors covered include Dickens, Smollett, Mark Twain, Dr Johnson, John Le Carré.
ISBN 1-871551-01-3; A5 size; 220pp; illus.

The Good That We Do *by John Lucas*
John Lucas' new book blends fiction, biography and social history in order to tell the story of the grandfather he never knew. Horace Kelly was born in Torquay in 1880 and died 60 years later, soon after the outbreak of World War II. Headteacher of a succession of elementary schools in impoverished areas of London during the first part of the 20th century, "Hod" Kelly was also a keen cricketer, a devotee of the music hall, and included among his friends the great Trade Union leader, Ernest Bevin. In telling the story of his life, Lucas has provided a fascinating range of insights into the lives of ordinary Londoners: their entertainments, domestic arrangements, experiences of the privations of war, including the aerial bombardments of 1917 and 1918, and their growing realisation during the 20s and 30s that they were doomed to suffer it all again. Threaded through is an account of such people's hunger for education, and of the different ways government, church and educational officialdom ministered to that hunger. *The Good That We Do* is both a study of one man and of a period when England changed, drastically and for ever.
ISBN 1-871551-54-4; A5 size, 213pp

In Pursuit of Lewis Carroll *by Raphael Shaberman*
Sherlock Holmes and the author uncover new evidence in their investigations into the mysterious life and writing of Lewis Carroll. They examine

published works by Carroll that have been overlooked by previous commentators. A newly discovered poem, almost certainly by Carroll, is published here. Amongst many aspects of Carroll's highly complex personality, this book explores his relationship with his parents, numerous child friends, and the formidable Mrs Liddell, mother of the immortal Alice. ISBN 1-871551-13-7; 70% A4 size; 118pp; illus.

Laughter in the Dark – The Plays of Joe Orton *by Arthur Burke*
Arthur Burke examines the two facets of Joe Orton. Orton the playwright had a rare ability to delight and shock audiences with such outrageous farces as *Loot* and *What the Butler Saw*. Orton the man was a promiscuous homosexual caught up in a destructive relationship with a jealous and violent older man. In this study – often as irreverent as the plays themselves – Burke dissects Orton's comedy and traces the connection between the lifestyle and the work. Previously a television critic and comedian, Arthur Burke is a writer and journalist. He has published articles not only on Orton but also on Harold Pinter, John Osborne and many other leading modern dramatists.
ISBN 1-981551-56-0; A5 size; 97pp

Liar! Liar!: Jack Kerouac – Novelist *by R.J. Ellis*
The fullest study of Jack Kerouac's fiction to date. It is the first book to devote an individual chapter to each and every one of his novels. *On the Road, Visions of Cody* and *The Subterraneans*, Kerouac's central masterpieces, are re-read indepth, in a new and exciting way. The books Kerouac himself saw as major elements of his spontaneous 'bop' odyssey, *Visions of Gerard* and *Doctor Sax*, are also strikingly reinterpreted, as are other, daringly innovative writings, like 'The Railroad Earth' and his "try at a spontaneous *Finnegans Wake*" – *Old Angel Midnight*. Undeservedly neglected writings, such as *Tristessa* and *Big Sur*, are also analysed, alongside better known novels like *Dharma Bums* and *Desolation Angels*. *Liar! Liar!* takes its title from the words of *Tristessa's* narrator, Jack, referring to himself. He also warns us 'I guess, I'm a liar, watch out!'. R.J. Ellis' study provocatively proposes that we need to take this warning seriously and, rather than reading Kerouac's novels simply as fictional versions of his life, focus just as much on the way the novels stand as variations on a series of ambiguously-represented themes: explorations of class, sexual identity, the French-Canadian Catholic confessional, and addiction in its hydra-headed modern forms. Ellis shows how Kerouac's deep anxieties in each of these arenas makes him an incisive commentator on his uncertain times and a bitingly honest self-critic, constantly attacking his narrators' 'vanities'.

R.J. Ellis is Professor of English and American Studies at the Nottingham Trent University. His commentaries on Beat writing have been frequently published, and his most recent book, a full modern edition of Harriet Wilson's *Our Nig*, the first ever novel by an African American woman, has been widely acclaimed.
ISBN 1-871551-53-6; A5 size; 295pp

Musical Offering *by Yolanthe Leigh*
In a series of vivid sketches, anecdotes and reflections, Yolanthe Leigh tells the story of her growing up in the Poland of the 30s and World War II. These are poignant episodes of a child's first encounters with both the enchantments and the cruelties of the world; and from a later time, stark memories of the brutality of the Nazi invasion, and the hardships of student life in Warsaw under the Occupation. But most of all, this is a record of inward development; passages of remarkable intensity and simplicity describe the girl's response to religion, to music, and to her discovery of philosophy.

The outcome is something unique, a book that eludes classification. In its own distinctive fashion, it creates a memorable picture of a highly perceptive and sensitive individual, set against a background of national tragedy.
ISBN 1-871551-46-3; A5 size; 57pp

Norman Cameron *by Warren Hope*
Cameron's poetry was admired by Auden, celebrated by Dylan Thomas and valued by Robert Graves. He was described by Martin Seymour-Smith as: "one of ... the most rewarding and pure poets of his generation ..." and is at last given a full length biography. This eminently sociable man, who had periods of darkness and despair, wrote little poetry by comparison with others of his time, but always of a high and consistent quality – imaginative and profound.
ISBN 1-871551-05-6; A5 size; 221pp; illus.

Shakespeare's Non-Dramatic Poetry *by Martin Seymour-Smith*
In this study, completed shortly before his death in 1998, Martin Seymour-Smith sheds fresh light on two very different groups of Shakespeare's non-dramatic poems: the early and conventional *Venus and Adonis* and *The Rape of Lucrece*, and the highly personal *Sonnets*. He explains the genesis of the first two in the genre of Ovidian narrative poetry in which a young Elizabethan man of letters was expected to excel, and which was highly popular. In the *Sonnets* (his 1963 old-spelling edition of which is being reissued by Greenwich Exchange) he traces the mental journey of a man

going through an acute psychological crisis as he faces up to the truth about his own unconventional sexuality.

It is a study which confronts those 'disagreeables' in the *Sonnets* which most critics have ignored.

ISBN 1-871551-22-6; A5 size; 84pp

Shakespeare's Sonnets *edited by Martin Seymour-Smith*
Martin Seymour-Smith's outstanding achievement lies in the field of literary biography and criticism. In 1963 he produced his comprehensive edition, in the old spelling, of *Shakespeare's Sonnets* (here revised and corrected by himself and Peter Davies in 1998). With its landmark introduction, it was praised by William Empson and John Dover Wilson. Stephen Spender said of him: "I greatly admire Martin Seymour-Smith for the independence of his views and the great interest of his mind" and both Robert Graves and Anthony Burgess described him as the leading critic of his time. His exegesis of the Sonnets remains unsurpassed.

ISBN 1-871551-38-2; A5 size; 200pp

POETRY
Adam's Thoughts in Winter *by Warren Hope*
Warren Hope's poems have appeared from time to time in a number of literary periodicals, pamphlets, and anthologies on both sides of the Atlantic. They appeal to lovers of poetry everywhere. His poems are brief, clear, frequently lyrical, characterised by wit, but often distinguished by tenderness. The poems gathered in this first book-length collection counter the brutalising ethos of contemporary life, speaking of and for the virtues of modesty, honesty, and gentleness in an individual, memorable way. Hope was born in Philadelphia where he raised his family and continues to live near there. He is the author of critical studies of Shakespeare and Larkin and is the biographer of Norman Cameron, the British poet and translator.

ISBN 1-871551-40-4; A5 size; 47pp

Baudelaire: Les Fleurs du Mal in English Verse
translated by F.W. Leakey
Selected poems from *Les Fleurs du Mal* are translated with parallel French texts and designed to be read with pleasure by readers who have no French, as well as those practised in the French language.

F.W. Leakey is Emeritus Professor of French in the University of London. As a scholar, critic and teacher he has specialised in the work of Baudelaire for 50 years. He has published a number of books on Baudelaire.

ISBN 1-871551-10-2; A5 size; 153pp

Lines from the Stone Age *by Sean Haldane*
Reviewing Sean Haldane's 1992 volume *Desire in Belfast* Robert Nye wrote in *The Times* that "Haldane can be sure of his place among the English poets." The fact that his early volumes appeared in Canada and that he has earned his living by means other than literature have meant that this place is not yet a conspicuous one, although his poems have always had their circle of readers. The 60 previously unpublished poems of *Lines from the Stone Age* – "lines of longing, terror, pride, lust and pain" – may widen this circle.
ISBN 1-871551-39-0; A5 size; 53pp

Wilderness *by Martin Seymour-Smith*
This is Seymour-Smith's first publication of his poetry for more than 20 years. This collection of 36 poems is a fearless account of an inner life of love, frustration, guilt, laughter and the celebration of others. Best known to the general public as the author of the controversial and best selling *Hardy* (1994).
ISBN 1-871551-08-0; A5 size; 52pp

PHILOSOPHY
Deals and Ideals *by James Daly*
Alasdair MacIntyre writes of this book: "In his excellent earlier book *Marx: Justice and Dialectic* James Daly identified Marx's place in and extraordinary contribution to the moral debates of the modern era. Now he has put us even further in his debt not only by relating Marx to his Aristotelian predecessors and to the natural law tradition, but also by using this understanding of Marx to throw fresh light on the moral antagonism between Marx and individualist conceptions of human nature. This is a splendid sequel to his earlier work."
ISBN 1-87155-31-5; A5 size; 156pp

Marx: Justice and Dialectic *by James Daly*
Department of Scholastic Philosophy, Queen's University, Belfast.
James Daly shows the humane basis of Marx's thinking, rather than the imposed 'economic materialistic' views of many modern commentators. In particular he refutes the notion that for Marx, justice relates simply to the state of development of society at a particular time. Marx's views about justice and human relationships belong to the continuing traditions of moral thought in Europe.
ISBN 1-871551-28-5; A5 size; 144pp

The Philosophy of Whitehead *by T.E. Burke*
Department of Philosophy, University of Reading.
Dr Burke explores the main achievements of this philosopher, better known in the US than Britain. Whitehead, often remembered as Russell's tutor and collaborator on *Principia Mathematica,* was one of the few who had a grasp of relativity and its possible implications. His philosophical writings reflect his profound knowledge of mathematics and science. He was responsible for initiating process theology.
ISBN 1-871551-29-3; A5 size; 101pp

Questions of Platonism *by Ian Leask*
In a daring challenge to contemporary orthodoxy, Ian Leask subverts both Hegel and Heidegger by arguing for a radical re-evaluation of Platonism. Thus, while he traces a profoundly Platonic continuity between ancient Athens and 19th century Germany, the nature of this Platonism, he suggests, is neither 'totalizing' nor Hegelian but, instead, open-ended, 'incomplete' and oriented towards a divine goal beyond *logos* or any metaphysical structure. Such a re-evaluation exposes the deep anti-Platonism of Hegel's absolutizing of volitional subjectivity; it also confirms Schelling as true modern heir to the 'constitutive incompletion' of Plato and Plotinus. By providing a more nuanced approach - refusing to accept either Hegel's self-serving account of 'Platonism' or the (equally totalizing) post-Heideggerian inversion of this narrative – Leask demonstrates the continued relevance of a genuine, 'finite' Platonic quest. Ian Leask teaches in the Department of Scholastic Philosophy at the Queen's University of Belfast.
ISBN 1-871551-32-3; A5 size; 154pp

FICTION

The Case of the Scarlet Woman – Sherlock Holmes and the Occult
by Watkin Jones
A haunted house, a mysterious kidnapping and a poet's demonic visions are just the beginnings of three connected cases that lead Sherlock Holmes into confrontation with the infamous black magician Aleister Crowley and, more sinisterly, his scorned Scarlet Woman.

The fact that Dr Watson did not publish details of these investigations is perhaps testament to the unspoken fear he and Holmes harboured for the supernatural. *The Case of the Scarlet Woman* convinced them both that some things cannot be explained by cold logic.
ISBN 1-871551-14-5; A5 size; 124pp

MISCELLANEOUS
Music Hall Warriors: A history of the Variety Artistes Federation
by Peter Honri

This is an unique and fascinating history of how vaudeville artistes formed the first effective actors' trade union in 1906 and then battled with the powerful owners of music halls to obtain fairer contracts. The story continues with the VAF dealing with performing rights, radio, and the advent of television. Peter Honri is the fourth generation of a vaudeville family. The book has a foreword by the Right Honourable John Major MP when he was Prime Minister – his father was a founder member of the VAF.
ISBN 1-871551-06-4; A4 size; 140pp; illus.